Leading Schools
in Disruptive Times

*For our families and staff, without whom
this work would not have happened*

Leading Schools in Disruptive Times

How to Survive Hyper-Change

Dwight L. Carter

Mark White

A Joint Publication

CORWIN
A SAGE Publishing Company

FOR INFORMATION:

Corwin

A SAGE Company

2455 Teller Road

Thousand Oaks, California 91320

(800) 233-9936

www.corwin.com

SAGE Publications Ltd.

1 Oliver's Yard

55 City Road

London EC1Y 1SP

United Kingdom

SAGE Publications India Pvt. Ltd.

B 1/I 1 Mohan Cooperative Industrial Area

Mathura Road, New Delhi 110 044

India

SAGE Publications Asia-Pacific Pte. Ltd.

3 Church Street

#10-04 Samsung Hub

Singapore 049483

Publisher: Arnis Burvikovs

Senior Associate Editor: Desirée A. Bartlett

Editorial Assistant: Kaitlyn Irwin

Production Editor: Tori Mirsadjadi

Copy Editor: Megan Granger

Typesetter: C&M Digitals (P) Ltd.

Proofreader: Jeff Bryant

Indexer: Joan Shapiro

Cover Designer: Anupama Krishnan

Marketing Manager: Nicole Franks

Printed in the United States of America

ISBN: 978-1-5063-8431-3

This book is printed on acid-free paper.

Certified Chain of Custody
SUSTAINABLE FORESTRY INITIATIVE
Promoting Sustainable Forestry
www.sfiprogram.org
SFI-01268

SFI label applies to text stock

17 18 19 20 21 10 9 8 7 6 5 4 3 2 1

Contents

Preface

FROM *A NATION AT RISK* TO COLUMBINE TO TWITTER

In 1983, I sat in my car and listened to a story on National Public Radio about the newly released education report sending tremors through American public education. Though I was a young, beginning teacher, I knew this was a seminal moment in education. "Our nation is at risk . . ." the report stated. I sensed I was about to be swept up in a wave of change that would transform American education.

I was right, but I could not have imagined the full impact of that report or the other disruptions, from Columbine to Twitter, that would rattle the education world over the next 35 years. I saw changes that led to more changes. Like other school administrators, I noticed that the changes seemed to be arriving more frequently. We moved from *A Nation at Risk* to No Child Left Behind to Race to the Top to the Every Student Succeeds Act. The computers sped up, became cheaper, and appeared in more classrooms. Smartphones created a world of opportunity—and apps, and challenges—for school leaders.

Schools have become more complex, and leadership job descriptions are becoming longer and more detailed. Many of the 20th century responsibilities are still present: School leaders must still lead orderly schools, take care of the students and staff, and be accountable to parents. But in the 21st century I've seen the challenges of managing social media, maintaining student safety, promoting diversity, leading multiple generations, providing transparency, implementing constant school reforms, and getting students global-ready.

THE RATE OF CHANGE IS GROWING EXPONENTIALLY

In the 20th century I could cope with an issue and quickly move on to the next one; it was a simpler time. But I noticed in the 21st century I had to cope with more difficult issues, rapidly adjust my operations to prepare for the next disruption, and then work with my staff to transform mindsets to understand what was happening. On too many occasions, today's school leaders cope with disruptions without taking the time to analyze or reflect on the changes rattling their schools. Thus, they're not prepared for the next viral video or social media storm.

It's not because of a lack of effort on their part. On the contrary, school administrators are some of the most capable and hardest working leaders in the world. They have worked in an environment with constantly shifting expectations and shrinking budgets while dealing with the greatest disruptions in global history. The economy and society have been shifting rapidly in the past three decades, and school leaders have been charged with keeping up with them. But the world has changed so rapidly it's hard to comprehend it all.

THE GOALS OF THIS BOOK

This book will help you

- see the history of American school disruptions as a lens through which to understand what is happening in schools today,

- recognize the major disruptions that are reshaping our schools and use them to transform your thinking and that of your staff,

- use a new model for charting school progress, one built around 21st century disruptions and not just a 20th century assessment system, and

- look to the future to see the radical changes coming so you will be prepared to meet them.

After reading this book, you will have a deeper understanding of

- why disruptions are affecting our schools,
- how to more effectively identify and manage disruptions,
- a new evaluation system that more effectively measures what schools accomplish, and
- ideas for transitioning your schools into hyper-change.

SPECIAL FEATURES

The book is unique in several ways.

- **Scope:** It provides a broad look at the disruptions of American school history to help the reader understand the scope of what is happening today.
- **Practical Ideas:** The book then helps leaders narrow the focus to identify the disruptions affecting their own schools through practical ideas at the end of each chapter.
- **Stories From Exceptional Educational Leaders:** Some of the finest educators have contributed their ideas and stories to this book; they are all award-winning, highly respected, experienced educators. They provide real-life, authentic tips to which all school leaders can relate.
- **Decision-Making Framework:** A new decision-making framework designed around coping, adjusting, and transforming is offered that specifically targets 21st century disruptions.
- **A New Model of Leadership:** Most leadership books espouse honing leadership skills within the current education model; this book promotes the idea that school leadership must be improved to prepare for the next model that will be brought about by hyper-change.
- **A Glimpse Into the Future:** The book offers ideas of what education might look like within the next 15 years as artificial intelligence makes education a differentiated, interactive experience for all students—and what leaders can do now to shift their own thinking and that of their staff.

- **End-of-Chapter Tips:** Chapters end with practical actions school leaders can take to implement the suggestions discussed in the chapters.

- **Scenarios for Applying the CAT Strategy:** Each chapter offers scenarios for school leaders to help them apply the CAT strategy (coping, adjusting, and transforming) introduced in Chapter 2.

- **Activities:** Each chapter contains useful activities school leaders can engage in with their staff to practice leading in disruption.

This shift in thinking is not optional; our schools will cease to exist within the next two decades if we don't take these steps. The disruptions entering our schools will continue to accelerate; school leaders must rapidly pivot to a new problem-solving model designed around coping, adjusting, and transforming.

I have the highest respect for school leaders and the challenges they face on a daily basis and through the span of their careers. I hope this book can help them.

Mark White
@markwhite55

with

Dwight Carter
@Dwight_Carter

Acknowledgments

We'd like to thank the many people who made this book possible and worked with us through the years as we sought new paths through education. First is Superintendent Gregg Morris, who hired us both to be administrators in the Gahanna-Jefferson Public Schools in Gahanna, Ohio, and contributed his ideas to this book. Gregg gave us the freedom to grow and implement new ideas as principals, and he has left a lasting legacy in the community and in our careers. Another great administrator featured in this book is Charles Rouse, the long-time principal of Leander High School in Leander, Texas. Today the district has Charles Rouse High School, named in his honor, and when it comes to having a positive impact on teachers and young people, no one's ever been better.

We've truly been honored to have an incredible group of educators offer their anecdotes and insights in the chapters about the various disruptions. They are award-winning superintendents, principals, and teachers who are at the top of their profession and took hours of their time to answer our questions and come along on this journey with us. Each day they shape the world for their students, and through this book they are helping positively impact thousands of other educators and students. Thanks to Aleta (Ebrett) Adams; Angie Adrean; Keith Bell; Meegan Bennett; Paul C. Dols; Dr. Jay R. Dostal; Patrick Gallaway; Dr. Kevin Grawer; Carrie Jackson; Jack M. Jose; Chris Lehmann; Brandi Lust; David Manning; Jason Markey; Derek McCoy; Dr. Jennifer Regelski; Michael John Roe, EdD; Gary Sebach, AIA; Ira Sharfin; Krista L. Taylor; Kate Thoma; Todd A. Walker, PhD; Rae L. White, PhD; William L. Wittman; and Steve Woolf, PhD.

We are grateful to Arnis Burvikovs and Desirée Bartlett at Corwin Press for their ideas and patience. They've understood that we, too, are still practicing administrators and our time and energy are carefully parceled out to myriad projects. They helped us stay on path through this one, and it was all done with professionalism and, most important, kindness.

We'd like to thank our families for their patience as we spent countless hours at school events, were on the road consulting, or were locked away in our studies writing for hours at a time. While they might not have their names on the cover, this book would not have been written without their understanding.

Finally, we give our thanks to the thousands of teachers and students with whom we have interacted in the past three decades. Their actions, ideas, and support have shaped us as leaders and educators. They showed us there's no finer place to spend a career than in a school. We hope this book helps them as they transition into the next stage of school development.

PUBLISHER'S ACKNOWLEDGMENTS

Corwin gratefully acknowledges the contributions of the following reviewers:

David G. Daniels, High School Principal
Susquehanna Valley High School
Conklin, NY

Virginia E. Kelsen, Executive Director, Career Readiness
Chaffey Joint Union High School District
Ontario, CA

Delsia Malone, Principal
W. E. Striplin Elementary School
Gadsden, AL

Nancy M. Moga, K–5 Principal
Callaghan Elementary School
Covington, VA

Sandie Morgan, 6–8 Math and 8 Religion Classroom Teacher
Nativity of Mary School
Independence, MO

About the Authors

Dwight L. Carter and Mark White have worked together for over 15 years, first in the Gahanna-Jefferson Public Schools in Gahanna, Ohio, where they were both administrators, and now as authors, speakers, and consultants. Together they led a team of teachers, students, and community members in the design of Clark Hall, a high school building that was named the Best in Tech 2012 by Scholastic because of its innovative use of global skills, technology, and learning space to teach Generation Z. They coauthored (with Clark Hall architect Gary Sebach) *What's in Your Space? 5 Steps for Better School and Classroom Design* (Corwin Press). They have a passion for working with other educators to help unlock the secrets of teaching today's young people, and they continue to write and explore new topics, especially those concerning 21st century school leadership. They both live in the Columbus, Ohio, area.

Dwight L. Carter

Dwight is the principal of New Albany High School in New Albany, Ohio. Prior to accepting this position, he was the principal of Gahanna Lincoln High School in Gahanna, Ohio. In 2013 he was named a national Digital Principal of the Year by the National Association of Secondary School Principals (NASSP). He is also an inductee in the Renaissance National Hall of Fame because of his incredible work in developing positive student culture. Dwight has frequently been a guest speaker in schools, universities, and at local, state, and national conferences that deal with Generation Z, technology use, staff development, school culture, and other 21st century education topics. He has authored numerous blogs and has written on behalf of NASSP. During his 22-year career, he has also been a high school social studies teacher, a high school assistant principal, and a middle school principal.

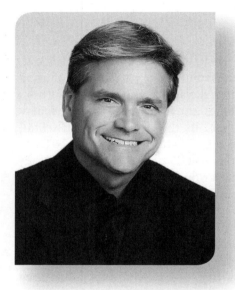

Mark White

Mark is a school leader, author, and consultant. He was previously the director of education and outreach at Mindset Digital in Columbus, Ohio, the academic principal at the Beijing National Day School in Beijing, China, and the superintendent of the Gahanna-Jefferson Public Schools in Gahanna, Ohio. During his tenure as superintendent, the district earned the state's highest academic rating and implemented a wide variety of global skills and technology into its curriculum, and he was a member of the Dell Platinum Advisory Council. During his 35-year career, Mark has been a consultant to both the College Board and ACT and has served on two national education reform committees. He has frequently been a guest speaker in universities and at local, state, and national conferences. Prior to being a superintendent, Mark was a high school English teacher and department head, high school assistant principal, principal, and assistant superintendent.

Schools Disrupted

Understanding How We Got Here

SOME BACKGROUND

To begin to understand what is happening in schools today, let's go back to the 1960s. It was a different era, the one that helped shape today's eldest school leaders, the baby boomers. The United States had entered the Space Race, and politicians had begun their call for a heavier emphasis on math and science in public schools; they were laying the first bricks in the long road of school accountability. Massive computers that filled entire rooms spat out formulas for satellites and lunar modules. African Americans were marching for civil rights. Television was still in black and white, and communication to the masses came via television and radio. Parents learned about their children's progress through handwritten report cards brought home three or four times each year, and when they wanted to speak to a teacher, they called and left a message with the school's front office or attended the open house held in the fall of each school year. Anyone could walk into any school any day through any door—which was almost always unlocked. Public school graduates often found jobs in the local community, and the American economy dominated the world. Young people had the same dreams as their parents: to become educated, get good jobs, and live the same types of lives as those who had come before them. In summary, American schools looked and operated as they had done for many decades, some might say for the previous century.

Those were simpler times for school leaders. An administrator could take a job as a building principal or superintendent with the knowledge that the school and district would probably be operating in much the same way in the future as they were in the present—and perhaps for the rest of that administrator's career. Even though technology was advancing and civil rights views were shifting in the 1950s, '60s, and '70s, changes in school operations came at a slower pace that was much more manageable and predictable. This is not to say these were easy jobs; some of these leaders dealt with extreme pressures in their schools, struggling with alcohol and drug issues, race relations, and antiwar protests. And they had the challenges of helping students, parents, and teachers navigate through the usual travails of youth and adolescence.

But that was before

- the Internet changed the world;
- school reforms brought massive amounts of testing;
- social media became a way for anyone to share a message;
- the middle class moved to the suburbs, leaving impoverished students in the urban schools;
- parents could e-mail teachers or contact them through Twitter or Facebook pages;
- Columbine and Sandy Hook changed how we view student safety;
- the global economy transformed the workplace and began to create a global society; and
- millennials dominated the workforce and Gen Z arrived with its own set of dreams.

We live in a world that is now being disrupted on many fronts, and those disruptions are buffeting our schools. Technology is advancing, social mores continue to transform, and today's educator leaders struggle with 21st century disruptions that were incomprehensible to their predecessors in the 20th century.

Some of the old challenges are still found in today's schools, but they have become bigger and more visible to the entire world. For example, 20th century administrators might have dealt with a racial altercation in a school and managed the repercussions in their community; that same racial altercation today can be broadcast on social media, and people on the other side of the world can watch it and discuss it. Parents in the 20th century might have complained about a teacher or administrator by signing a paper petition and attending a school board meeting; today the petition will be online 24/7, with photos, videos, and comments—and it could be covered by the local television news with a link to a website formed by the parental group.

There are more challenges now. Social media, globalization, LGBTQ equality issues, transparency, and generational differences are new 21st century disruptions that have made school leadership jobs more complex. It's no coincidence 50% of American school principals now leave their schools within 3 years of starting their positions ("CHURN: The High Cost of Principal Turnover"). They either leave on their own or are pushed out the door by teachers or parents who are demanding more than the principals are capable of achieving.

How did school leadership jobs become so huge, and what can administrators do to more effectively manage them? If principals are going to thrive in the 21st century, and if their schools are going to survive as viable educational entities, they must

- understand how American education became so disrupted;
- develop a new method to cope, adjust, and transform in a constantly shifting environment;
- take a broader view of how they are evaluating their progress; and
- begin to look to the future as even more impactful disruptions arrive at faster rates.

To transition from surviving to thriving, let's take a 30,000-foot view of the school disruption landscape to get a broader perspective on what's happening in schools today and what we as school leaders can do to address it.

SCHOOL ADMINISTRATORS ARE DEALING WITH AN OVERLOAD OF INFORMATION AND DEMANDS

Principals and superintendents have so much data and so many demands coming at them each day that it's difficult to keep up.

Many of them have reached the point where they know they just can't do it all anymore.

The futurist Alvin Toffler saw it coming. In 1970, he became famous with the publication of his best-selling book *Future Shock*, which he said is "the shattering stress and disorientation that we induce in individuals by subjecting them to too much change in too short of a time" (Toffler). He said the world was about to enter an amazing new age in which we would see massive societal and economic transformations, a rapid acceleration in change, and life beginning to move "faster and faster—in everything from technology to family structure to politics" (Toffler). He said people would be "moving more, throwing away their belongings sooner and having to adapt more often to new kinds of work" (Kaste).

These ideas will sound familiar to educators; they are leading schools today as Toffler predicted almost 50 years ago. Schools now deal with perplexing changes in new family structures, advancing technology, and an evolving global economy. The data are coming at schools in bigger batches, so much that it's overwhelming. Personal technology continues to evolve more quickly than school technology. Societal mores are shifting to the point that debates rage about topics ranging from Internet freedom-of-speech issues to who can use which school restrooms; for better or for worse, what has been accepted in schools for 100 years could be changed today with a White House directive.

As we speak with principals and superintendents, we hear of the stress they endure on a daily basis. They want to be successful. They are trying to chart a path into the unknown without clear directions—while being held in the stranglehold of a 20th century school model designed for the Industrial Age.

Some school leaders are open to new ideas. The more progressive principals and superintendents want to

- stress more creativity and other global skills in classrooms, but they must devote most of their efforts to raising test scores because of their heavy weighting in accountability ratings and job security;

- break out of the 9-month school years to try new calendars, but their communities want to hold on to the traditional calendars because those are the ones they know; and

- reallocate funding into different areas for new initiatives, but the political uproar from stakeholders who see cuts to their long-established programs would be too intense to withstand.

And as they try to break out of the traditional mold, they are still consumed by the tasks of managing parent, student, and staff needs and taking care of the multitude of other issues that fill their daily agendas.

The politicians who demand that educators prepare their students for a 21st century world are often confining them with reduced funding, more 20th century thinking, and a vision that doesn't extend beyond the next election cycle. Contrast their environments with those of business executives who recognize they must pivot quickly to new operating procedures if their firms are to survive; school leaders are locked into systems that are slow to react and made more cumbersome by the need to placate a wide range of special interests, including the locally elected school board, which might have various political agendas. How many Fortune 500 firms would thrive in a system where they had to elect members of the local community to approve all their long-term strategic decisions, hire the leaders, and be the ultimate authority in resolving problems, even when those decision makers had no prior experience in that field? Yet this is the system in which school leaders work.

If schools are to move forward with the accelerations of the 21st century, then the leaders must deploy new coping methods and strategies. They must move from a state of future shock to a state of future awareness.

THE THIRD WAVE OF HISTORY IS FUELING RAPID DISRUPTIONS IN OUR SCHOOLS

In 1980, Toffler (and his coauthor/wife, Heidi Toffler) published *The Third Wave*, in which they stated we were looking at world history from the wrong angle. Instead of viewing it in decades, centuries, or eras, we should step back and take an even wider look—and see that world history is moving in waves.

The first wave of history was the longest, the 10,000-year Agrarian Age, when people lived off the land and technology advances slowly transformed parts of the world. When the first schools were established in the American colonies, the first wave was reaching its end. Most people in the colonies made their living on small farms, and the schools that existed used curriculum, instruction, and assessment methods that had been consistently deployed for hundreds of years in Europe for those students fortunate enough to receive an education. Students were released from learning for the summer months. The standard of education quality varied widely from school to school based on the instruction and stability of the teacher and the environment, but the rate of educational change was the slowest in our history.

The Tofflers assert that the second wave of history began with the Industrial Revolution in England in the late 18th century. It began to transform the United States in the early 19th century. Our rural schools operated as they had in the past in the traditional one-room schoolhouse, while some urban schools began to grow in size. The seeds of disruption began to take root. Horace Mann of Massachusetts gained national prominence in the 1830s with his call for high-quality, free public education, and the first kindergarten was opened in Wisconsin in 1856. The National Teachers Association (now the NEA) was founded in 1857, and Charles Darwin published his (still) controversial *Origin of Species* in 1859. The Department of Education was established in Washington, D.C., in 1867 to promote education. During this period, some schools were opened for African Americans, with perhaps the most famous being Booker T. Washington's school in Tuskegee, Alabama, in 1881. The future of student writing would eventually be transformed by an invention in 1884: the fountain pen (Sass).

In the early 20th century, the disruptions began a slight acceleration and their impact became more profound. Both John Dewey and Jean Piaget released their ideas on learning, the American Federation of Teachers was founded, and the SAT was administered for the first time. In 1938 Franklin Roosevelt signed an act that set a minimum age for working in non-agricultural jobs and limited the number of hours and types of employment for older children (Sass).

But note the amount of time that passed between these disruptions; educational change was slow to arrive and limited in its impact. When the Second Industrial Revolution accelerated in the last part of the 19th century and early part of the 20th century, one could still step into a classroom and find many of the same materials and methods as had been employed in George Washington's time. In other words, the first two waves of history washed over American schools, and the education methods barely shifted. Yes, the nation and society had undergone dramatic changes, but schools had not.

They didn't need to adjust.

The skills taught in schools in the first and second waves of history could allow graduates to be successful in agrarian and industrial societies. What had worked in the 1700s would work well into the 1900s. Since most people in that time span either worked on farms or did repetitive tasks in factories or offices, there was no strict mandate for educational change to teach application skills. While some schools went through isolated disruptions because of growth or changes in the teacher workforce and turnover, for the most part the schools were stable. Leading schools or teaching then wasn't easy; it's always been hard. Educators in those times faced daunting challenges, but the educational changes were slower to arrive.

Then the advances of the industrial wave reached their apex during World War II. Albert Einstein and some of the greatest minds of the Industrial Age worked to split the atom and create the first nuclear bombs in World War II, but the case can be made that a number of disruptions being felt in American schools today rippled out of Pearl Harbor in 1941. In addition to splitting the atom, the other revolutionary disruptions we (and our British allies and German adversaries) created were plastics, jet engines, rockets, new types of metals, penicillin, radar, new methods of electronic communication, a better understanding of mass transportation, and increased systems of production on a broad scale. The German missile system formed the foundation of America's early space program in the 1950s and 1960s, which led to an increase in computing capability and other forms of new technology (Finnamore and Ludlow).

In the late 1940s, as American servicemen and -women were mustered out of the service and returned home to a changed world, a few intrepid people began to look around and ask, "What should be taught in our schools now?"

The choir of disruption was beginning its song.

In the 1950s, as Americans were led by Dwight Eisenhower and claimed the title of leaders of the Free World, our society and schools were rocked by one of the most significant, and most necessary, disruptions in our history: the *Brown v. Board of Education* case of 1954. Freedom meant equality, and what was happening in Topeka, Kansas, suddenly impacted every public school system in the United States. Education leaders began to ask how they would integrate schools and deal with the conversations, tensions, and promise of fulfilling the role of American schools for all their students.

Then, as the civil rights movement began to escalate and accelerate, American school leaders were pulled into the front lines of the Cold War. The Soviets were the first into space in 1957 when they launched their *Sputnik* satellite, and perplexed politicians turned their eyes on public school leaders for answers (Powell). We suddenly had a missile gap to close with the communists, and Congress said it was up to educators to do it. The call went out for more mathematics and sciences.

American schools received a large share of the blame for a national political problem, and it led to broad attempts to significantly restructure their operations. The American education system was now center stage and bathed in a red-white-and-blue spotlight—and it has not been switched off since.

Across the United States, school principals and superintendents, predominantly white males, probably went home in the evenings, sat in front of their black-and-white television sets eating frozen dinners off of TV trays, and said to their wives, "You know, I don't understand what's happening. It used to be things were so much easier."

Goodbye, stability. Hello, disruption.

And hello to the third wave of history. The Tofflers said the Industrial Age was receding in the second half of the 20th century, and the rise of computers would bring about the Information Age, when knowledge would be found more quickly and success would go to those who understood that the world had shifted and who could apply new ideas.

Educators will recognize the major points of *The Third Wave* that have led to disruptions in schools, such as

- the rise of individualism;

- a growing difficulty in reaching consensus;

- a breakdown in many standardized factory models;

- new ways of producing thought, products, and wealth; and

- a move away from mass media to a growth in ideas shared by individuals and small groups.

In schools today, we see more individual expressionism from students than ever before, and their ideas are often expressed through social media and with online images and videos. Parents are pushing back in growing numbers against the standardized testing models of the Industrial Age. Current graduates are no longer fully accepting the ideals of the past, that they must attend college to get a good job and settle down, get married and have kids at a young age. Instead they want to chart their own paths, create new apps, balance work and leisure, and use technology to solve many of their problems. They are looking for new ways to be productive and to be happy. People have, as Toffler predicted, moved away from mass media to sharing ideas in public media, which can be done through Facebook, Snapchat, Twitter, and other social media platforms.

As we move forward, school leaders should understand American education disruptions are not isolated events; they are tied to this new wave of history. School leaders were trained in a second-wave model, but the third wave requires an adaptive mindset and new ways of viewing the world and how to educate students to thrive in it.

SCHOOLS HAVE EXPERIENCED THEIR OWN WAVES OF CHANGE; AMERICAN SCHOOLS ARE ENTERING THE FIFTH WAVE OF THEIR DEVELOPMENT

For administrators to fully understand the disruptions in schools today, they should apply the Tofflers' wave theory to education. The Tofflers saw three waves of global history; we can see five waves of American school history: three that have already occurred, a fourth wave that is just ending, and a fifth wave that is now rising out of the accelerations around us. When we view our professional history through waves, it allows us to comprehend what is happening now—and what we must do as 21st century school leaders to thrive in the next wave.

Five Waves of American School History

Wave 1—Stability Age: 1600s to mid-1940s

Wave 2—Nuclear Age: 1945 to 1980

Wave 3—Accountability Age: 1983 to 1999

Wave 4—Disruption Age: 1999 to Present

Wave 5—Hyper-Change Age

The first wave came ashore in the 13 colonies with the European settlers, who brought their respect for education and the idea that learned individuals could teach a roomful of attentive students the fundamentals of knowledge. The teacher was the center of learning. All assignments, instructions, and classroom functions originated with the adult in front of the room, and disruptions were slow to arrive and minor in scope. As mentioned earlier, this concept was central in our schools until just after World War II. From the time of the founding fathers to the fathers of baby boomers, American education was relatively unchanged and stable—schools were anchored in a **Stability Age** that lasted from the 1600s to the mid-1940s.

That wave ended at 5:29:45 a.m. on July 16, 1945, when the United States detonated the world's first nuclear bomb in the Arizona desert. The advances in technology reached new levels with the splitting of the atom, which resulted in a shifting in education expectations. In this second wave of American school history, people began to understand that schools had to start adjusting to a world in which science had accelerated and society was transforming. This was the **Nuclear Age** of American schools, the 1950s, '60s, and '70s, when American life was dominated by nuclear reactors, the Cold War, spaceships, highways, cars, televisions, refrigerators, microwaves, and shopping malls. Schools promoted democratic/capitalistic ideals and were desegregated by forced busing and then resegregated when middle-class families moved to the suburbs. Teachers and principals were rocked by the societal shifts that included the civil rights movement, two wars against communism, the peace movement, hippies, illegal drugs, and a deep questioning of traditional values. Educators tore down some of the classroom walls to create open classrooms—and then put them back up when they couldn't see much of a difference in results.

To find the spot where the second wave crashed to its end and the third wave began, we need to move from Arizona to Washington, D.C., where *A Nation at Risk* was released in April of 1983. The global economy was on the rise in Mexico, India, and Europe, and seeds of doubt began to take hold about the effectiveness of American schools. Suddenly, we were being told the future of our nation depended on our ability to reform schools through heavier doses of standardized testing. In one state capital after another, legislators implemented piles of assessments and accountability ratings. The **Accountability Age** was upon us; we wanted to test our way to greatness.

For the next 16 years, American educators dutifully complied with the new requirements. We shifted curriculum outcomes, developed standards and assessments, and began to adapt a mindset of change. We were safely ensconced in our buildings, aligning lesson plans to standards and preparing for the next round of testing. Then American education changed in a single day on April 20, 1999, at Columbine High School in Littleton, Colorado, when two students massacred twelve students and one teacher. Who would have thought one horrible incident could have such a wide and sudden impact? Within 24 hours, schools locked their doors forever and began hiring school resource officers and planning lockdown drills. Everyone began to ask, "What if it happened here?" We would never feel so safe again; our world had been violently disrupted, and this would be just the first of numerous types of disruptions that would rock education culture and schools: accelerated education reforms, 9/11 and terrorism, the advent of social media, the founding of charter schools, the deep impact of the Internet on teaching and learning, the emphasis on mental health problems among students—and the list goes on. This is the age in which we live now, the fourth wave of American school history:

the **Disruption Age.** The disruptions are not stopping; we will not begin a school year in the future and find the disruptions have calmed and we can take a break from our shifting mindsets. They are coming at us more quickly.

To get a wider picture of the various disruptions that have reshaped schools, consider the reforms, technology, and shifts that have entered schools since the 1980s (Figure 1.1).

FIGURE 1.1 The Increase in School Disruptions by Decade

1980s	1990s	SINCE 2000
• *A Nation at Risk*	• The Internet	• No Child Left Behind
• Mass testing	• The global economy	• Subgroups
• Copy machines placed in workrooms	• Standards-based curricula	• Smartphones
• Middle-class flight to the suburbs continues	• Accountability ratings	• Texting
	• Distance learning	• Facebook
	• Websites	• Twitter
	• Personal computers	• LinkedIn
	• E-mail	• Periscope
	• Voice mail	• YouTube
	• Computer games	• Viral videos
	• Columbine	• iPods
		• Tablets
		• Blended learning
		• Vouchers
		• Charter schools
		• Changes in the SAT
		• Changes in the ACT
		• Common Core State Standards
		• Increased testing
		• More parent access
		• Calls for more school transparency
		• Heightened political scrutiny
		• The 2008 recession

LEADING SCHOOLS IN DISRUPTIVE TIMES

1980s	1990s	SINCE 2000
		• State funding cuts
		• Race to the Top
		• Wearable technology
		• Student and parent mental health concerns
		• Sandy Hook
		• Every Student Succeeds Act
		• Millennials enter the teaching ranks
		• Gen Z enters schools
		• More diversity issues

Administrators who feel their world has accelerated are right; in the past three decades the disruptions have reshaped their jobs. Today's principals and superintendents are experiencing change at a level unimaginable to their predecessors.

And when we look at the overall history of American school disruptions, we can see the accelerations of the past 30 years are the most sweeping in American school history (see Figure 1.2).

The amount of change administrators are experiencing in schools is not imagined or exaggerated; the disruptions are accelerating, and their jobs are accelerating with them.

If we look closely at the pace of disruptions around us, we can see we are beginning the fifth wave of American school change: the **Hyper-Change Age**. How is hyper-change different from other change? It is faster and deeper. Not only do the changes arrive at faster rates, but they are stacked on top of changes in new areas that might not have existed a decade ago. For example, social media assumed its prominent spot in society and schools 10 years ago, but new apps and extensions are constantly being introduced and then adopted by students. Educators have learned to log on to Facebook and Twitter—as students have switched to Snapchat and

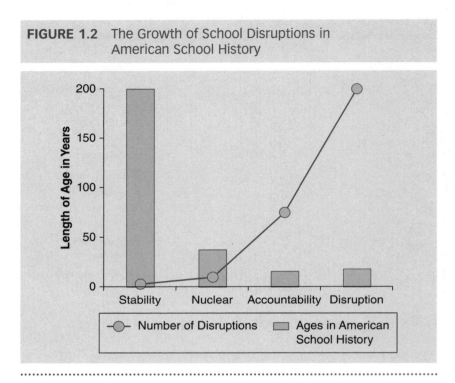

FIGURE 1.2 The Growth of School Disruptions in American School History

Pinterest. As we strive to understand a new disruption, the latest iteration arrives and we are forced to shift again. And education reforms continue to arrive at faster paces, bringing broader curricula, more testing, and greater accountability measures.

As school leaders, we want students to have the skills to pass their tests. But those of us leading schools today understand that education in an era of disruption and hyper-change is wider than standardized testing: We are already coping with accelerations in school safety, technology, diversity, generational differences, inequality, transparency, and globalization. While we are evaluated by test scores, these other areas are already deeply embedded in our schools and operations. It's time for us to recognize them, deal with them more effectively, and assess our progress in these areas to get a truer picture of the quality of education. (A new assessment model will be discussed in Chapter 10, and hyper-change will be covered more deeply in Chapter 11.)

It's time to move leadership models from the 20th century neighborhood model to one designed for a global society.

PROCESSING SPEEDS HAVE FUELED TECHNOLOGY DISRUPTIONS AND CREATED A NEW EDUCATION LANDSCAPE

Sometimes school leaders are in awe of the technology used by students in their personal lives, of how young people can use an app to solve a problem or play an online game with someone in another state.

They also look at the speed of their students' phones. Or the newest high-tech camera systems being placed in schools. Or the flat-screen television being installed in the outer office. Or the latest Chromebooks in the classrooms that surf the Internet, stream music through a cloud service, allow students to create charts and videos, and let them access free websites that help them arrange images to tell a story. Personal devices are becoming more complex, and they are changing the trajectory of society and learning. Processing speeds have been doubling every two years; computing has been getting stronger, and knowledge is growing. Captain Kirk and the *Starship Enterprise* haven't docked in outer orbit yet, but they're in the neighborhood.

Gordon Moore saw the technology disruptions coming. After Toffler, he's the second futurist school leaders should study to understand the disruptions rocking our schools. He looked at what was happening with processing speeds in computers and created Moore's Law.

Ask your school IT person about Moore's Law, and he or she will probably get excited to the point of giggling and stammering about how Moore predicted in 1965—when the United States was still running on massive, gas-guzzling eight-cylinder Detroit engines—that we would all soon be running our lives on transistors, integrated circuits, and microprocessors that would double in speed every two years and change how society functioned. He originally said speed would double in a decade, but in 1975 he adjusted his time frame downward, saying it would actually double every 2 years for the next decade ("Moore's Law").

He was only partially right. The processing speeds did, indeed, double every 2 years for the next decade—but they continued to double every 2 years for the next *four* decades. Put another way, computing speed is hundreds of thousands of times faster today than it was in 1975. He saw it coming and got it right. For IT geeks, Moore is not just the cofounder of Intel who created a theory for processing speeds; he's a superhero. He's Captain America with an integrated circuit board strapped to his shield.

Students today are digital kids. They are part of Generation Z, and in many ways they are products of Moore's Law. They are connected to the Internet on the average of 9 hours each day (Wallace); they watch videos on their smartphones that are streamed from YouTube, Netflix, and Hulu; and they have access to more information at their fingertips than any other generation in history. It's hard to imagine the changes they'll see in their lifetime brought about by technology—or the wonderful technology that will be used to educate them in the future.

In 2015, Moore said we were reaching the saturation point for current semiconductor speeds and that the law would probably die out within the next decade or so. But the rate of change is not slowing down. It will not do so in our lifetime. Everyone who studies computing speeds says progress will continue (Waldrop).

Some researchers assert computers will begin to think like humans. Many educators are aware of the software created by Ray Kurzweil that can help students understand text; he has a startling prediction for the future:

> Many scientists believe the exponential growth in computing power leads inevitably to a future moment when computers will attain human-level intelligence: an event known as the "singularity." And according to some, the time is nigh.

> Physicist, author, and self-described "futurist" Ray Kurzweil has predicted that computers will come to par with humans within two decades. He told Time Magazine . . . that engineers will successfully reverse-engineer the human brain by the mid-2020s, and by the end of that decade, computers will be capable of human-level intelligence. (Wolchover)

We must prepare for an education world where teachers and students are assisted by human-like computers. The question is not if the technology disruptions will stop or if they will continue to transform education; the question is, "Will we have the adaptive mindset to stay ahead of new technology and find ways to apply it in our education systems?"

KNOWLEDGE IS DOUBLING AT FASTER RATES, WHICH IS REDEFINING EDUCATION

All this change has led struggling school leaders to think about what it means for students to be successfully educated in a world of hyper-change. In earlier waves of our school history, administrators could easily define what it meant to be educated. They could point to courses, credits, and a high school diploma. But processing speeds and a world with new expectations for education have made the old answers obsolete and have created questions about the purpose of education today.

A third futurist, Buckminster Fuller, has chronicled the growth of knowledge. School leaders should study the work of this futurist to get a better idea of how to educate students in this century.

A lot of bright people consider Fuller to have been one of the greatest thinkers of the 20th century. He was born in Milton, Massachusetts, in 1895, and he dedicated his life, and his enormous intellect, to thinking of how to help all mankind. In 1982 he published a book titled *Critical Path*, in which he charted the history of knowledge. According to his calculations, knowledge doubled in the world from the year 0 to 1500. Then it began to speed up: It doubled again by 1750, and then again by 1900. When World War II ended 45 years later, knowledge had doubled again and it continued to accelerate until now, when it doubles every 12 or 13 months—which means every year we now have twice the amount of knowledge we had the year before (Schilling).

The doubling of knowledge will continue to accelerate. An IBM Big Data Study released in 2012 foresees a day in the future when knowledge will double every 12 hours (Schilling). For young people, this means there will be twice as much knowledge available at the end of each school day, and twice as much again when they wake up the next morning. And it will keep doubling . . . and doubling . . . and doubling.

This leads to some serious questions for educators: How many textbooks should we be purchasing today when they are becoming obsolete faster than ever before? How much memorization should students do in an age when information is growing so rapidly or is at their fingertips?

Or when we can pull facts out of the air?

We already have phones and other devices that are voice activated and give us information ranging from weather reports to historical data. All we have to do is talk to them, and they answer us. Like other technology, this form will deepen in the future, become cheaper, and assume a more prevalent role in our lives. This new era calls for new ways for students to access information; we have to do more to provide online access to students so they will have the most up-to-date information at their fingertips.

Consider the chart in Figure 1.3, which shows how processing speeds have led to the growth of knowledge, which has led to the incredible technology advances we are seeing today. Technology in schools is not an option; it's a necessity. It must be the new foundation of learning.

FIGURE 1.3   The Correlation of Processing Speeds and Knowledge Growth

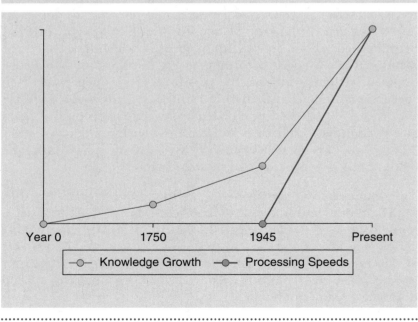

LEADING SCHOOLS IN DISRUPTIVE TIMES

IF SCHOOL LEADERS ARE GOING TO THRIVE, THEY MUST USE DISRUPTIONS TO THEIR ADVANTAGE

School leaders must pull these points together to understand why their environments have shifted and what they must do to move forward:

1. The Tofflers say history moves in waves, and we have entered the third wave of history, one where knowledge and individualism rule.

2. American school history is also moving in waves; we are in the fourth wave, the Disruption Wave, and we are entering the fifth, the Hyper-Change Wave.

3. Gordon Moore predicted the increase in computer speeds, which has resulted in an explosion of knowledge and more technology in our schools.

4. Buckminster Fuller looked at the growth of knowledge; it's doubling so quickly that current education systems are struggling to keep pace.

Education leaders must recognize what is happening, constantly adapt to a changing environment, and use the disruptions to their advantage.

How can school leaders do this? In the Understanding by Design (UbD) framework, we speak of keeping the end in mind and finding the essential questions to clarify our thoughts. Today, as technology continues to expand and knowledge doubles more rapidly, the essential question is not about test scores or district accountability ratings. The essential question for educators to answer is: **What does it mean to be educated in the 21st century?**

The Tofflers assert that the transition period when one wave is ending and the new one is beginning is often the most difficult because we tend to view the world through the lens with which we are most comfortable, the one we already know (Toffler and Toffler). The world might be changing, but if we are still looking through yesterday's lens, we will not see what is occurring today. We will search for what we know and find it has transformed or is no longer visible.

This is where we are in education today, in the middle of a conflict between the old and the new. The second wave of machines is giving way to the third wave of technology and accelerated change. While some school leaders recognize what is happening, too many of them still cling to the past and attempt to lead their schools through the most turbulent of waters with second-wave ideas.

Here's the critical epiphany for school leaders: We can drown between the waves—or we can grab 21st century surfboards and start riding the new one. We can't predict everything about the future, but because of the knowledge explosion and the advances in technology, we know school leaders will have to understand and adapt to disruptions to surf the new wave.

If they are going to surf, they will have to build a new sort of leadership surfboard with three critical parts.

The New Leadership Surfboard

Part I: The Academic System

Will help students

- adjust socially, vocationally, and academically in an age of disruption;

- apply knowledge in constantly shifting environments; and

- prepare for hyper-change, where the world at the end of their lives will be very different from the world into which they were born.

Part II: An Adaptive Mindset

Will help leaders

- plan beyond a 9-month school year to help them envision what education can be 5 and 10 years into the future, and

- understand today's schools don't have to look like the ones from the past, that educators should build learning spaces for today's students and not the students of the past century.

Part III: The Steering Fin

Will guide school leaders' thinking to

- know that past disruptions led to present disruptions, which will lead to future disruptions;

- embrace change and the unknown—to be comfortable with being uncomfortable;

- understand that school disruptions are an unending part of their careers;

- cope with disruptive events in the hours after they occur, adjust their mindsets in the months following the disruptive events, and transform their long-term philosophy and actions around that disruption and future disruptive events; and

- gaze into the future and predict the approaching disruptions— before the disruptions upend their schools.

More than anything, school leaders must maneuver their surfboards to the front edge of the third wave. They must accept disruptions and then use them to the school's advantage to maximize education in the 21st century. That's what this book is meant to be: a way to build a surfboard and help school leaders move from the back of the wave—or from the rough trough between the waves— to the crest of the third wave of history.

As educators, we espouse lifelong learning for our students. The same applies to our school leaders; they will be learning for the rest of their careers. The days of mastering the profession are over; the days of constant adaptation are upon us. The ability to cope, adjust, and transform through disruptions will determine whether school leaders will remain relevant or be relegated to a few paragraphs of online history books. Their future is in their hands—as is their ability to develop a new mindset to lead their schools in disruptive times.

ACTIVITIES TO TRANSITION TO 21ST CENTURY LEADERSHIP AND HYPER-CHANGE

Tasks of the 20th Century Leader vs. the 21st Century Leader

List the percentage of your time on a yearly basis you spend on the following tasks that range from the typical management duties to proactive 21st century leadership. Your percentages should add up to 100.

TASKS OF THE 20TH CENTURY LEADER	PERCENTAGE OF TIME SPENT ON TASK DURING A TYPICAL DAY	NOTES
Helping students with personal, discipline, or other school issues		
Communicating with stakeholders through face-to-face conversations, phone calls, e-mail, or social media		
Managing staff issues		
Managing budget issues		
Planning professional development		
Studying data		
Leading professional development		
Other 20th century leadership tasks of your job:		
TASKS OF THE 21TH CENTURY LEADER	**PERCENTAGE OF TIME SPENT ON TASK DURING A TYPICAL DAY**	**NOTES**
Implementing global skills into the curriculum		

TASKS OF THE 21ST CENTURY LEADER	PERCENTAGE OF TIME SPENT ON TASK DURING A TYPICAL DAY	NOTES
Studying how to prepare students to enter the global economy		
Planning ways to get technology into the hands of young people to use in their education		
Exploring ways to use social media to advance the school's message and image		
Employing initiatives that strengthen bonds between diverse groups in the school		
Finding new ways to enhance communication with parents		
Looking for proactive ways to improve student safety at school		
Implementing mental health initiatives for students and parents		
Understanding how millennial teachers think and how they are influencing the staff		
Researching Gen Z students and how they learn		
Designing new types of learning space and operations for Gen Z		
Sharing new ideas with staff to help them shift their thinking		

(Continued)

(Continued)

TASKS OF THE 21ST CENTURY LEADER	PERCENTAGE OF TIME SPENT ON TASK DURING A TYPICAL DAY	NOTES
Studying societal and district trends to understand and predict future disruptions		
Other local global leadership tasks of the job:		
Total percentage of time should equal 100.		

What do you notice about your time spent in each category? Do you wish you could spend more time in the 21st century domains?

Ideally, in which particular domain(s) would you spend most of your time?

If you are like many school leaders today, you probably are spending the majority of your time in 20th century categories—because those are still critical areas that must be addressed. But a goal should be to move more into the 21st century leader categories. It might not be done overnight, and it might be difficult with all the tasks that continue to take your time, but knowing those categories are there is part of moving from a state of future shock to a state of future awareness.

Types of School Disruptions
New Problems Going Viral

The definition of insanity is doing the same thing over and over and expecting different results.

—Often attributed to Albert Einstein

One of the definitions of sanity is to tell the real from the unreal. Soon we'll need a new definition.

—Alvin Toffler

Albert Einstein and Alvin Toffler were two of the great thought leaders of the 20th century, and their views of insanity and sanity are indicative of the decades in which they lived. Einstein was at his most famous in the years following World War II, when the first shudders of disruption were felt in American schools, and Toffler's most famous writing was done in the latter part of the century, when the shudders had become waves that shook American schools and continue to pummel them today. These two philosophers can both be seen as correct in their views of sanity and insanity; school leaders should consider both definitions as they lead schools into hyper-change. Insanity for school leaders will be if they approach change in the 21st century in the same way they approached change in the 20th century and if they fail to recognize that what is unreal today is about to be real within the next 20 years as hyper-change redefines education.

They will need to recognize what is happening around them and constantly shift their mindsets. Old ways of thinking must always be questioned, and new realities must be quickly accepted.

One school leader who has done this is Gregg Morris; he has spent over 46 years in education, with 40 of those years being spent as a superintendent who has successfully navigated through disruptions. In 2012, Morris was named the Ohio Superintendent of the Year. One reason he's thrived is his flexibility. He has some advice for today's school leaders and those entering the profession in this era of rapid change: "If you have any areas in which you have to stay exactly the same or can't get in sync with the times, then you're going to be miserable!"

When asked about the changes he's encountered through the decades, Morris begins by discussing the changes he's seen in young people:

> It's different today, and kids are different today. It isn't easy being a kid. I think there are so many things pulling at them. The alcohol, the drug culture, and addiction issues are so prevalent today. Kids have expectations to grow up immediately. They get into structured programs early that should be fun, but it starts a pressure cycle. There are a lot of temptations, and kids feel so infallible. Social media has changed the world. Kids used to meet at malls. Now they meet through social media.

One of the great disruptions in American schools has been the fear of violence and the need to maintain student safety, and Morris has seen the evolution from the pre-Columbine days to the present:

> The old model was just to do nine fire drills each year. Now safety training is part of our staff development. Our teachers are trained to handle almost any crisis. We've had two major evacuations of our schools just in the past year. When something bad happens at school, the kids send it

out before we get out of the building and the parents are already lined up outside the school. You used to send a note home and get it back. Now parents are online talking about it.

Morris has also led through four decades of change in instruction and seen the impact of standardized testing:

The way we teach kids has really changed. We used to be so segmented. We had a lot of pieces of knowledge that didn't fit together. We didn't understand how everything connected. I suspect the agrarian/industrial society had something to do with that; kids could come out of high school and earn a living and raise a family without a high school diploma because it didn't mean that much. It's different now.

What the state has done with testing has probably made us better, but it's been a weak implementation. The important part is we now assess kids and learn where they are and base our teaching on the results. We can go back and reteach and go for mastery, so we do a better job with that than we used to do. Our teachers today really grasp how to deal with differences in the kids and how to reach kids. Kids don't fall through the gaps so often. We're helping struggling kids more.

But overall the state testing is overkill—it's a journey that never ends. We've gone through three changes in tests in the past three years. There's too much emphasis on it. Teachers can't be as creative as they used to be.

According to Morris, two other huge issues have risen out of the disruptions: Society has become more litigious, especially with schools, and parents want instant answers. "I have to have more access to the school attorney than I did 30 or 40 years ago," he said, "and parents are in the online grade book—and when they ask a question they want an answer back that evening!"

If school leaders are to survive in the 21st century, they must do what Gregg Morris has done: They must constantly look at the shifting educational landscape and see what is happening.

UNDERSTANDING DISRUPTIONS AND DISRUPTIVE EVENTS

The cable network CNBC released a list in 2015 of the 50 companies that are reshaping life in the United States; they are disrupting our views and operations in society (CNBC). Educators will recognize at least four of them: Uber, Airbnb, Dropbox, and Survey Monkey. When educators go to conferences, they might use Uber instead of a taxi to get to their hotel—that is, if they are going to a hotel and haven't rented a house or apartment through Airbnb. At the conference, they might take notes and upload them to their Dropbox accounts so they won't ever be lost, and on the way out the door they could be given a link to Survey Monkey so the facilitators can get feedback on the conference. All these companies have created new ways of doing things and are putting intense pressure on the long-established companies in their fields.

Schools, like traditional firms, are being buffeted by disruptions. Educators need to understand this:

- A **disruption** is any invention or societal shift that *gradually* changes how schools operate.

- A **disruptive event** is an incident based on a disruption that *suddenly* changes how schools operate.

INTRODUCING THE CAT STRATEGY: COPING, ADJUSTING, AND TRANSFORMING

The key to successfully dealing with change in the 21st century, especially the sudden disruptive events that often are sprung on schools without warning, is to implement adaptive mindsets in staff and to use a solving framework built around coping, adjusting, and transforming (CAT). In the CAT framework, school leaders do the following:

1. Recognize the disruptive event and **cope** with it immediately. When a crisis occurs, the goal is to peacefully resolve it as quickly as possible, usually within hours or days of its inception.

2. **Adjust** school policies and operating procedures in the days and weeks after the incident to prevent its reoccurrence or to handle it and other disruptions more efficiently.

3. Continue to **transform** their philosophies and school cultures through study and reflection in the months after the incident so that their thought processes and adaptive strategies will be deepened in the future.

When school leaders in the 20th century managed disruptive issues, they could usually just cope with them and move on without reflecting on the issues, because they tended to be narrower in scope—and they weren't transmitted to the world for public consumption. The complexities of today's disruptions and their potential for recurring and deep harm to school cultures and individuals require school leaders to constantly adjust their operating procedure and constantly work with their staff to transform their mindsets and school culture. The times are changing rapidly, and the problems are becoming bigger. The days of reaction are over; today's administrators must be more proactive than they have been in the past.

Many leaders today don't take the time to study the scope of the viral video, the characteristics of Gen Z or millennial parents, or the reason a disruptive event has occurred. Because of their lack of understanding or time constraints, principals and superintendents don't take the time to adjust and transform; they just cope. Thus, they often have recurring issues in schools that they don't comprehend or fail to adequately address.

IDENTIFYING THE SEVEN DISRUPTIONS CHANGING SCHOOLS TODAY

Consider the following list of seven major disruptions that have changed almost every school in the United States. School leaders have been dealing with them for at least a decade, and they can tell stories about the impact each disruption has had, both positive and negative, on their schools and careers. Each disruption has brought disruptive events that have helped shape individual school cultures and led to significant changes in how schools operate and are led today. Individually, they are challenging; collectively, they amount to a tsunami of change.

Seven Major Disruptions
Our Schools Face Today

1. The emphasis on **student safety**, including the fear of school shootings, the laser-like focus on social/emotional development, and efforts to combat high stress levels in today's students and families

2. Accelerating **technology** advances that change how students learn and how schools operate, including the influx of smartphones, wearable technology, and the impact of social media

3. A sequence of **reform efforts** such as *A Nation at Risk*, No Child Left Behind, Common Core State Standards, and the Every Student Succeeds Act that have resulted in complex school accountability ratings that drive instruction, learning, hiring practices, and budgeting

4. The **generational challenges** that occur when baby boomers, Gen Xers, Gen Yers, and millennials work together in the teaching force, and the demands of Gen Z that are leading to new types of teaching methods and learning spaces

5. The explosion of knowledge and getting students **global ready**, including the challenge of teaching global skills in a rigid, test-driven curriculum and attempting to answer the question, "What does it mean to be educated in the 21st century?"

6. Dealing with increasingly complex **diversity** issues, including racial tension, ethnic differences, political polarization, and LGBTQ issues

7. The growing demand for **transparency** by parents who want access to school information, including 24-hour access to student grades; their demand for prompt responses from educators to their questions and demands; and their constant examination of the school's curriculum, clubs, and overall goals

---

FINDING THE DISRUPTIONS IN THEIR OWN SCHOOLS

School leaders can begin their transformation by identifying the disruptions and disruptive events that have had the greatest impact on their schools in the past decade. Each school has its own story to tell—and its own path to the future.

While the seven greatest disruptions have been significant in both their breadth and depth, some schools have been affected by other disruptions unique to their communities. For example, a disruption might occur if a major employer in a town goes out of business, resulting in mass unemployment, shifts in the population, and a reduction in tax funding, which will have dire consequences for the local schools. Or a political change on the local school board could lead to positive or negative disruptive events. While politics are a part of every public school and some private schools, they sometimes interfere with the mission of education. Perhaps leadership changes at the principal or superintendent level have affected the district's or school's trajectory. Educators can often point to the hiring or departure of a key leader and say, "That's when things really started to get better . . ." or "That's when we started our decline. . . ."

Myriad other issues could also fall into the "other" category, such as helping students with discipline and emotional issues, resolving custodial questions, dealing with personnel problems, working with demanding parents, and resolving all the other issues that are often confronted on a daily basis. They are all demanding and tremendously time-consuming.

The activity at the end of Chapter 1 asked administrators to study their allocation of time and energy. If all the disruptions were equal in their impact and time needed to deal with them, a chart depicting them would look like Figure 2.1.

FIGURE 2.1 An Equal Distribution of Time and Energy Managing Disruptions

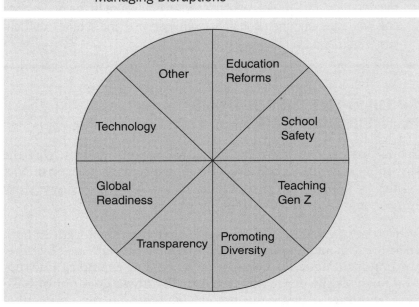

However, the impact of the disruptions on school operations is not equal. In many schools, administrators spend much of their time managing education reforms (such as doing teacher evaluations and preparing for standardized testing) and resolving issues in the "other" category. A reproportioned chart to show where administrators spend their time on many days might look like Figure 2.2.

On too many days, administrators find their time and efforts consumed by school safety and student discipline issues, which means there are a few days when the chart might look like Figure 2.3.

When administrators are forced to spend a great amount of time and energy on discipline issues and safety concerns, it takes away from the amount of progress that can be made educating Gen Z, training teachers to get students global ready, and promoting diversity in the student body to enrich the learning experience for everyone.

School leaders can begin their transition by asking questions like, "In how many days is the majority of time spent managing school

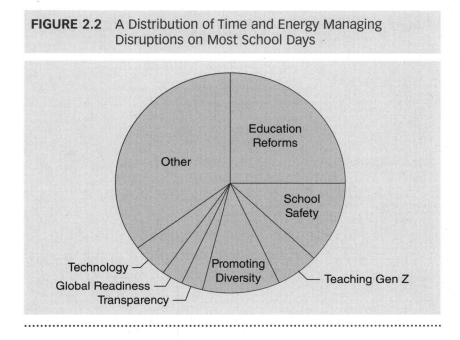

FIGURE 2.2 A Distribution of Time and Energy Managing Disruptions on Most School Days

safety and discipline issues?" and "If I could make one chart to represent the time and energy spent per category over the course of this entire school year, how would it look?"

And perhaps the most crucial question would be, "To move my school forward in the 21st century, how would I want my chart to look? How much time would I spend in each category based on the growth of my school in that category? How can I make my chart look more like my vision?"

All schools are different in their growth and needs, which means the charts from different schools could be slightly different. Finding the right mix is the challenge; it's part of the art of leadership in an age of disruption.

FORMING A VISION FOR A NEW TYPE OF LEADER: THE LOCAL GLOBAL LEADER

It used to be school controversies were local, but today the Internet, social media, and 24-hour websites have allowed any story to

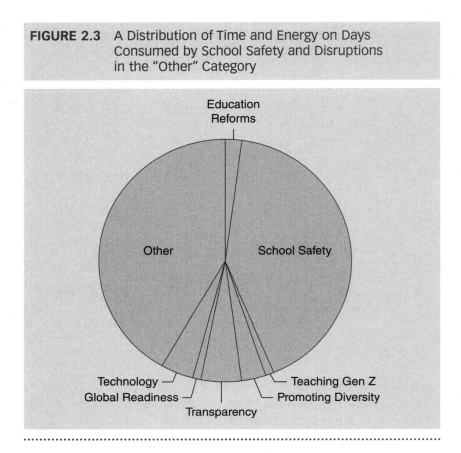

FIGURE 2.3 A Distribution of Time and Energy on Days Consumed by School Safety and Disruptions in the "Other" Category

become national or international news, which means school leaders must navigate the politics and policies of the local community while understanding that any action taken can potentially reach a global audience.

The Disruption Age has brought about the need for a new type of school leader: *the local global leader,* a leader who can maintain the traditional roles of school leadership while firmly understanding 21st century disruptions. A school leader's domain used to extend to the edge of the enrollment boundaries; a local global leader today must ascend to the highest peaks of the Information Age to obtain a global perspective—and then land softly in the school courtyard to patiently share the vision with students, parents, and staff. While we still might have neighborhood schools with deep histories and traditions, their mission is now global.

Thus, the leader's voice has been transformed from addressing local concerns to also preparing students to thrive in a global society.

The local global leaders use these disruptions to their advantage; the leaders who don't comprehend the disruptions spend their careers bouncing from crisis to crisis and wondering why they are occurring—because their thinking patterns are stuck in the 20th century leadership model. They don't have to be millennials to adjust to the new landscape. It's not a matter of age or experience; it's about widening their view and being brave enough to venture into new areas.

EXAMINING ACCOUNTABILITY THROUGH A 21ST CENTURY LENS

Most state accountability systems today are geared toward tests scores, graduation rates, attendance rates, and various other measurable categories. While these domains are still relevant, to focus exclusively on them and not the areas of disruption is to view progress through a 20th century window when a 21st century magnifying glass is needed.

School leaders should still examine their test scores and other accountability measures being used by the state, but they should also be asking key questions centered on the other disruptions in their schools:

- What is being done to prepare students to thrive in the global economy?

- What advances has the school made in how its teachers use technology and, just as important, how it is letting its students use technology? This includes classroom technology, social media, wearable technology, and other applications.

- What is the school doing proactively to create an inclusive environment and to minimize diversity issues?

- What is the school doing to minimize achievement gaps among subgroups and to create a culture in which students want to attend and not consider other education options?

- How is the school allowing parents to access information about their students and the school without overwhelming staff members?

- What steps have been taken to keep students safe while creating friendly learning space that promotes creativity and freedom of thought?

- How has the school adjusted to millennials in its workforce, to Gen Z learning styles, and to the need to examine learning space to meet the needs of today's world?

Answering these questions could lead to a stronger and more accurate 21st century school accountability system. In hyper-change, schools can no longer focus too heavily on test scores; they will have to expand their view of what they are accomplishing in their most disrupted areas. (More on this topic will be covered in Chapter 10.)

LOOKING TO THE FUTURE

For the past two centuries, school leaders have been asked to lead schools that prepared their students for entry into relatively stable, predictable societies and workforces. But that began to change with the advent of the Information Age and the emergence of the global economy.

Educator leaders must now spot trends, brainstorm, study what futurists are saying; *they should try to look into the next decade and beyond to guess what is waiting there.* Can they be completely accurate? No. Even the greatest futurists cannot predict every societal or global shift. But school leaders will have the greatest chance of visualizing future education needs and reforming their schools today if they can open their mindsets, reinvent operating procedures, and prepare their students and staff for a world that is just beyond the horizon.

We stand in the first year of the future; the coming decade can be seen through a haze that we have the ability to blow away with the winds of progressive thinking and action. It doesn't take a crystal ball; it just takes imagination, hard work, and the willingness to change. We don't need long-term plans, just long-term philosophies of adaptation. Author Seth Godin says, "A ten year plan is absurd; impossible, not particularly a waste of time. On the other hand, a ten-year *commitment* is precisely what is required if you want to be sure to make an impact" (emphasis added).

Here's a key point for school leaders to move forward in an age of disruption and hyper-change: It used to be school leaders could learn their craft in the first few years of leading and use those same methods for the rest of their careers—but those days are gone and are never coming back. While there will be some leadership commonalities that carry over from the 20th to the 21st century, this era calls for constant adaptation to a changing school landscape. And it's about more than having a growth mindset or an adaptive mindset; it's also about having a *positive* mindset, an "I can do this" attitude that gets them over the barriers and into the future.

These are amazing times to lead schools. While we are staring at the greatest disruptions to ever strike our schools, these disruptions also provide the greatest educational potential in history. Author and leadership expert Simon Sinek states in *Leaders Eat Last: Why Some Teams Pull Together and Others Don't*, "Leadership takes work. It takes time and energy. The effects are not always easily measured and they are not always immediate. Leadership is always a commitment to human beings." Working within and through these disruptions requires a commitment to serving others in ways that are not always quantifiable but are felt by all stakeholders. To this end, the need to feel valued in the Disruption Age is among the highest needs of human beings. Yes, leadership takes a great deal of responsibility and it is not to be taken lightly, but school leadership is still one of the most vital and rewarding of all fields.

We have no choice; we must adapt to this opportunity. Educators need to make sure learners in the 22nd century don't study articles about the demise of our education system because they weren't flexible enough to survive and tap into the disruptions. The future will belong to graduates who can apply knowledge effectively; in schools the future will belong to school leaders who recognize disruptions and seize the opportunity to use them to their advantage.

ACTIVITIES TO HELP UNDERSTAND SCHOOL DISRUPTIONS

Understanding Disruptions and Disruptive Events

1. Have you been forced to cope with a disruptive event? Did you have to adapt policies or operating procedures afterward? Did it transform your thought process in the long term to be more proactive in dealing with disruptions?

Viewing School Disruptions Through Decades

2. What are some of the major disruptions you've experienced during your career as an educator?

Recognizing the Seven Greatest Disruptions Affecting Schools Today

3. If you have been an educator for over 10 years, what have been the greatest changes you've seen in students, schools, and society?

4. What disruptions have caused some of the greatest "aha moments" for you in the past few years?

Finding the Disruptions in Your School

5. What are some of the greatest disruptions to affect your school in the past two decades?

6. What are some examples of positive disruptive events you have seen in your school?

7. What are some examples of negative disruptive events you have seen in your school?

8. Are there other disruptions in the past two decades you would add to the list that have dramatically altered the way your school operates?

Becoming a Local Global Leader

9. What have you done to become a local global leader?

10. Are your thought patterns and actions stuck in the 20th century, or have they moved to the 21st century?

Viewing Accountability Through a 21st Century Lens

11. What is being done in your school to prepare students to thrive in the global economy?

12. What advances has the school made in how its teachers use technology and, just as important, how it is letting its students use technology? This includes classroom technology, social media, wearable technology, and other applications.

13. What is the school doing proactively to create an inclusive environment and to minimize diversity issues?

14. What is the school doing to minimize achievement gaps among subgroups and to create a culture in which students want to attend and not consider other education options?

15. How is the school allowing parents to access information about their students and the school without overwhelming staff members?

16. What steps have been taken to keep students safe while creating a friendly learning space that promotes creativity and freedom of thought?

17. How has the district adjusted to millennials in its workforce, to Gen Z learning styles, and to the need to examine learning space to meet the needs of today's world?

Seeing the Future

18. Consider these two quotes and how they relate to your role as a 21st century educator:

    Alvin Toffler: "The illiterate of the 21st century will not be those who cannot read and write, but those who cannot learn, unlearn, and relearn" (*Future Shock*).

(Continued)

(Continued)

> Sir Ken Robinson: "Our task is to educate [our students'] whole being so they can face the future. We may not see the future, but they will and our job is to help them make something of it" (*The Element*).

How could you adjust your school's curriculum, instruction, and assessment to help students "learn, unlearn, and relearn"? What adjustments need to be made in the school culture? How do you help your students face the future?

Student Safety

From Innocence to the Unimaginable

For school administrators who have been in education for the past 20 years, their careers can be divided into two parts: before Columbine and after Columbine. This disruption added a whole new element of concern to the lives of principals and superintendents.

Many Americans forget that schools used to be welcoming places where the doors were propped open for any parent or community member to stroll through at any time. The local schools were red-bricked bastions of wholesomeness where the American flag fluttered on a massive flagpole in the front courtyard and where kids were taught the same subjects their parents had been taught, often in the same way. Their stability and calm sense of place were unquestioned. There might be an occasional fight from time to time in the secondary schools, but the idea of someone purposely entering with an assault rifle to kill as many students as quickly as possible just didn't exist.

It was too horrible to imagine.

Now we know otherwise. While the flag still flies in the front, our schools have become metaphors for American society: They were built in another time and now constantly adjust their policies to remain safe in a rapidly changing world. If you want to see a mirror of America, visit its public schools. The doors are locked and visitors push a button, look into a camera, and speak into a microphone to gain entry. Students practice lockdown drills where they barricade the doors to their classrooms and prepare to climb out windows. A suspicious package inadvertently left in a restroom can trigger an evacuation. Even the most rebellious student knows the consequence of saying he wants to bomb a school. Across America, naïve students have faced expulsion hearings for midnight tweets in which they jokingly wished someone would shoot up the school—preferably before their test the next day. They quickly found that student safety is no laughing matter.

In the schools where backpacks are still allowed, nervous middle school and high school administrators watch their students enter each morning and hope this is not the day one of them enters with a gun, knife, or bomb they learned to make on the Internet. Administrators go to work each day knowing their careers could be quickly altered or finished if they miss a clue or fail to adequately respond to a remark or suspicious activity. They are held accountable daily for the safety of their students and staff.

School principals and superintendents who left the profession prior to April 20, 1999, when Columbine occurred, have never known such daily pressure.

And there are other safety and health issues that have recently entered the job descriptions of school administrators. We know the danger of concussions, so we have protocols for helping students heal through them. Programs have been developed that can help identify students who are at risk of self-harm and suicide, so we try to find ways to safely implement them. Eating disorders are more commonly recognized and discussed than in the past, and we assist parents who are desperately seeking answers on how to help their kids. The full impact of bullying has been brought out into the open; many states have enacted laws that mandate certain procedures be followed when addressing bullying allegations, both the traditional type that takes place in the school cafeteria and the new sinister, 24/7 version: cyberbullying. Whenever any type of mental health or safety concern is identified, a fresh call goes out for schools to help deal with it. It's natural for parents and the rest of society to plea for help from the institution where young people spend their days, and educators invariably want to help.

But the resources are stretched thin, and the accountability measures in academics and the other areas of disruption make it increasingly difficult to successfully take on new responsibilities. It's not a matter of heart or effort for the administrators; they want to help. It's a question of time, money, and energy.

A PRINCIPAL'S VIEW OF STUDENT SAFETY IN 21ST CENTURY EDUCATION

One of the principals who knows of the challenges of leading safe schools in 21st century America is Dr. Kevin Grawer, the highly respected principal of Maplewood Richmond Heights High School in St. Louis, Missouri. Here are some of his observations about drills, evacuations—and the importance of knowing your students.

Stories From Exceptional Educational Leaders

Dr. Kevin Grawer, Principal
Maplewood Richmond Heights High School
St. Louis, Missouri

Schools are a social experiment and mirror society in a smaller setting. A few societal safety concerns have seriously changed since I entered the profession. For one, sadly enough, school shootings have become an event all school leaders must plan for. We tend to overemphasize the practice of fire drills, but most school deaths are the result of school shooters. Our school has invested in partnering with local police, staff, parents, and students to have frank discussions about what we would do in the event a school shooter entered our space. Philosophies have changed as recently as the past 5 years in the strategic plans for school shooters. In the past, students and staff were told to lock the door, turn out the lights, hide in the corner (as if no one was in the room), don't make a sound, and hope the shooter passes by the room. Well, we still

(Continued)

(Continued)

adhere to many of these philosophies, but we also tell students to grab anything that can be a weapon, barricade doors, and attack if the shooter enters the room. Studies show that distracting the shooter and attacking actually saves lives. We are not "sitting ducks" is what I tell our students and staff. We also plan to evacuate the building as quickly as possible even if the shooter is in the building (in another location). We practice exiting with police as quickly and smoothly as possible. Many schools also do mock shooter walk-throughs and study how to best deal with a school shooter in their space. These are difficult "run-throughs" but could be lifesaving in the event of an actual shooter. Because of this threat, controlling who enters our school space is much tighter. We have buzzers on entry doors and can monitor and control who enters and exits our school. We lock all entries after school starts, and doors remain locked all day.

While Grawer and his staff and students often drill for the occurrences within their schools, some of their greatest dangers originate beyond the school grounds and filter into the school. He points out the necessity today for school leaders to partner with students, parents, and law enforcement to maintain a safe environment.

Overall, I and most principals I speak with feel good about the general safety within our building space. The issues tend to come with things we simply cannot control that happen outside our school doors and then reverberate inside at some point. Many times incidents in the local community escalate and lead to further episodes within the school setting. Communication with local law enforcement outside of school hours is key, as is being in tune with student energy and moods. If we know a student is acting in a hostile or strange manner, hear disturbing rumors, we need to be proactive in getting to the root of the story before it ends up disrupting our school environment. This is when it is extremely important to know who your students are, who is likely to bring in outside issues, and how to proactively recognize them so our school day is undisturbed. I always say that there is nothing more important that we do than ensuring the smooth running of the school day. In order to do this, it takes a team of teachers, admins, counselors, school resource police officers, and support staff who know their kids and are willing to stop what they are doing to deal with urgent issues.

Incidents that occur outside our school day are external to our control, yet they have a major impact on our daily school lives. The student social media war that begins on Saturday night, the robbery of a student's home or car that happens at 8 p.m., the fight at a local park, or the crimes that occur in the neighborhood effect what happens the following days in school. Partnering with law enforcement, taking a proactive and aggressive stance in dealing with these issues, and promoting open communication with students and parents are integral to ensuring we have a safe day at school.

For example, if we have a shooting in the neighborhood and word gets around it may have involved a student or two from the school, we immediately partner with police and meet with all stakeholders and parents as soon as possible. If in any way this incident disrupts the school day, we remove the students from the school environment until we sort the entire case out. We would educationally create a plan for students if they are removed from school but never compromise the safety of the greater school for any reason.

Bullying: Moving From the Playground to Cyberspace

A strand of school safety that has grown more demanding of administrators' efforts is the prevention of and reaction to bullying. Grawer also has some interesting points to make about the wide parameters of harassment that fall under the new definition of school bullying and the importance of proactive measures that define and reinforce proper behaviors.

The mandate in our state declares that we must document and investigate any and all accusations of bullying. This even means that when a student sarcastically says, "He's bullying me," we are supposed to fill out the state-mandated (very tedious) bullying form.

Bullying itself has not changed much in the past 20 years, yet the parameters by which it has been defined have changed. Bullying in the past simply referred to someone using superior strength or influence to get someone else to do what they may not want to do. Now it refers to teasing, unwanted references on social media, physical intimidation or harassment (as it did in the past), criticism (warranted or unwarranted),

(Continued)

(Continued)

and really anything not wanted or sought by the apparent victim. Thus, when a student says, "He/she is bullying me," it can refer to a plethora of things.

We have not changed anything regarding our operations around dealing with bullying other than our documentation of it (as required by the state). As always, we spend more time modeling mutually respectful relationships, loving all our students, and letting kids know clearly what is "okay and not okay" in our space, and ensuring our consequences are quick, consistent, and known by all. This, for us, has been a key to limiting bullying in our school.

Improving Student Safety by Coping, Adjusting, and Transforming (CAT)

Occasionally, there will be security issues that cause leaders and staff members to take hard looks at their procedures. Grawer describes one incident in which students from another school gained access to his school and attacked a student in a classroom.

In the days following the intrusion, Grawer and his staff took immediate action to cope with the situation and try to prevent it from happening again.

To remedy this issue of unnoticed or unwanted visitors, we discussed means of fortifying our entrance system (locking all doors down). . . . We keep all school doors locked at all times now throughout the school day and after school.

Grawer knew they had to take the next step; they had to adjust their environment and procedures to develop a deeper, more effective method to keep intruders out of the school.

We also met with local police to discuss what to do in terms of defending our students and minimizing injury to all involved while getting law enforcement on the scene as soon as possible. We purchased a new buzzer entry system in all buildings (one way in, one way out). Finally, we partnered with local police to write a grant for interior and exterior cameras. We now have 80+ cameras on campus and those have made a huge difference from an administrative perspective.

School leaders used to deal with disruptive events through a 9-month school cycle. They could treat each event as a one-time occurrence and hope it didn't happen again. But now, with heightened concerns for student safety and the power of social media to increase the ramifications of each event, administrators must be thinking of school safety on a 12-month, 24/7 basis. To survive and prosper, school leaders must use these disruptive events as benchmarks in their transformational journeys. They must learn from each issue, deepen their reservoir of knowledge and responses, and be better prepared for the next disruptive event. In other words, they must continue to transform their thoughts, the philosophy of staff, and the proactive and reactive policies of the school.

Grawer understands this concept. Though the disruptive event was over and the school had returned to normal, he let the dust clear, stepped back, and worked with his staff to process what they had learned—and what could be done in the future to increase school safety.

Our staff certainly became more aware, informed, and uniform in our understanding of the procedures and policies we are taking to ensure the safety for all in our school. We have reviewed our safety policies each semester and do more intruder drills now than we have in the past. We used to place more emphasis on fire drills; however, now we tend to do more lockdowns and intruder drills, as they seem more relevant in 2017. I feel we are more prepared than ever for intruders and have a clearer system of dealing with intruders and active shooters. This does not mean we are immune to these types of events, but we know that we are better prepared for them.

Today, leaders must do more than just cope with the immediate aftermath of a safety event and hope it is not repeated, and they must do more than adjust their policies and operations. The leaders who understand 21st century disruptions will do a thorough job of transforming the thinking of their staff. They realize they live in rapidly changing times; adjustments might prepare them to meet the same threat in the future, but they must transform their thinking and philosophy *to be prepared for situations they have not yet seen*.

They, like Grawer, are making their local schools stronger because of their global perspective. They look at disruptive events and apply the CAT method (coping, adjusting, and transforming) repeatedly.

(Continued)

(Continued)

To summarize what Principal Grawer did:

- He and his staff coped with the disruptive event in the hours following the intrusion by reviewing what happened and ensuring their doors were locked.

- They adjusted their policies and environment in the weeks following the event by strengthening their bond with the local police, installing buzzer systems in all buildings, and writing a grant to fund installation of security cameras throughout the school.

- They transformed their philosophy and operations in the months following the event by layering more safety precautions (constant policy reviews and more intruder drills) into their culture. Policies and practices prepare a school to deal with the known threats, but a culture of awareness and precaution allows it to more effectively deal with new types of threats.

Mental Health: A Growing Priority

Mental health issues are also a key component of student safety, and schools have more responsibility than ever for providing assistance to struggling students and families. Grawer effectively summarizes what many school leaders are now encountering.

I think the health issues have always been there at schools, but we are more in tune with them now as they have become more and more widely accepted as legitimate issues in our greater society.

Mental health issues certainly have become a greater priority. I have attended sessions at academic conferences regarding mental health issues, read various articles, and conversed with other school leaders about what they are doing to serve their community's mental health needs. The fact that we offer mental health awareness sessions at principal's conferences speaks volumes about the impact it is having on our nation's schools. I am more skillful at finding supports for families and at being proactive in recognizing mental health needs among students. Often, I find that the mental health counseling for the student is not enough. In fact, the entire family needs to be involved in the process of counseling for a longer lasting impact for the student and overall family.

This is a greater challenge, as mental health issues are still not always recognized as "legitimate" among many families. Thus, they reject full family counseling, which in turn leads to a disintegrating family dynamic as communication becomes more challenging. It is sad to see a student struggle and parents not recognize the legitimacy of the struggle or, at times, overemphasize the struggle as a means to avoid attending to one's schoolwork or even attending school at all for that matter.

As with most schools, we have seen a rise in anxiety-related health concerns in the past few years. More and more students are receiving family-provided counseling outside of school to deal with their anxiety, depression, and mental-health-related issues. Whether it's in the form of self-harm (cutting) or in dealing with various stressors in one's life, our school has worked hard to support our students struggling in this area. We have partnered with a local social service organization (Preferred Family Healthcare), and they have provided us with a full-time counselor specializing in teen-related anxiety and social issues. This new counselor takes on a caseload and meets regularly with our students who opt in for this service. Our local community, in turn, has offered fully funded family support for families without insurance (or limited financial resources), thereby taking away any financial concerns they may have regarding mental health support.

Grawer makes an important point about addressing today's student mental health issues: Schools must examine their academic policies and seek to understand how they might be inadvertently creating stress for students.

Our staff, too, has had to learn how to deal with the rising stress-related issues among our students. We have had to look at our grading practices—deadlines, make-up work, and other related items—especially as related to our students experiencing severe anxiety/trauma symptoms. We have had to demonstrate flexibility in how we assess these students as well. We have taken advice from our counselors as to how to best assess each individual student based on their diagnosis and personal needs. This flexibility has been a result of multiple discussions among our staff with admins and counselors. Sometimes, we have to mandate from above what our staff needs to do, but mostly the teachers are very open to meeting the needs of the individual student.

(Continued)

(Continued)

We need to ensure that we have multiple points of entry for all mental health concerns in our school. By this I mean that we cannot rely on one sole counselor or teacher to be the "mental health" person in our school. Everyone takes a lead in connecting with students in need and guiding them to the proper support. We all need to be up to date on how to help families access what they need in order to better serve their children.

Schools used to not worry much about mental health issues. They often were not discussed, and when they were addressed the students were expected to fall in line and accept that adolescent stress in school was just a part of growing up. Now principals must lead their staff in finding ways to help young people, and superintendents are expected to create professional cultures where the student is more important than the curriculum or the grades.

It used to be the lone mental health expert in the school was the school nurse; she would spend most of her time in the clinic dealing with fevers, mumps, measles, and eye exams. Today, the nurse is aware of students who are having difficulties, but there are teams of people assisting students with mental health concerns. The most effective schools

- have partnerships with outside agencies,

- employ mental health counselors and social workers within the school,

- provide training for educators on the warning signs and the latest trends,

- are aware of the medication being taken by students to aid mental health, and

- actively reflect on what can be done to ease the stressors of young people.

Student mental health has become a disruption that will be addressed constantly by educators in the future, including the stressors that will be coming in the approaching age of hyper-change, whether the students are in school or being taught virtually. The world is not becoming less complicated; it is becoming more complicated.

A TEACHER'S VIEW OF STUDENT SAFETY IN 21ST CENTURY EDUCATION

Of course, teachers are also on the front lines of helping students with mental health concerns. An educator who eloquently sums up our challenges of school safety, bullying, and mental health is Paul Dols, a Renaissance Coordinator at Monrovia High School in Monrovia, California.

Stories From Exceptional Educational Leaders

Paul Dols, Renaissance Coordinator
Monrovia High School
Monrovia, California

I have had the honor and the privilege of being a classroom teacher for 21 years. It is a massive understatement to say that things have changed over the past two decades in my classroom, and in my school, and in our profession. I would hesitate to jump on the bandwagon of folks outside of education who look at our students today and lament how much "the kids have changed." I would argue that the kids haven't changed nearly as much as the world these kids live in has changed. Technology has completely flipped the world upside down when it comes to our kids. Many of the advances in technology are beneficial to students, and many are much more detrimental to their academic strength and their emotional wellness.

Dols remembers the school world before Columbine, and how schools changed so dramatically after Columbine.

When I became a teacher in the fall of 1995, the world was a different place. School safety was not on my radar at all as I entered my first classroom as a teacher. I was much more concerned with writing lesson plans, mastering classroom management strategies, and learning how to "survive" as a classroom teacher. The emotional well-being of my students has always been a priority for me, but I never thought of a school environment as being unsafe. Not as a student, and certainly not as a teacher.

(Continued)

(Continued)

Then Columbine happened. The tragic events of that April day in 1999 shocked all of us. I still remember my student Alfredo rushing into my classroom and telling me terrorists had taken over a school in Colorado and to put the TV on. That in itself tells you how safe we thought we were. The true horror came to light when it was announced that it was two students who had carried out this awful act. Columbine wasn't the first school shooting in our country, but for me it was the first realization that schools are not safety zones. Violence, anger, bitterness, and depression also find their way to our classrooms.

Since that fateful day in April, our country has seen more and more of these tragic events take place. In the back of my mind there is now always a concern for the safety of our school and, more important, the young people I am entrusted with each day. I believe it is important to note that it is almost always in the back of my mind. I am more conscious of suspicious behavior or students who are acting out of the ordinary. It is critical as educators that we know what ordinary is for each of our kids. It is one of the reasons developing a personal relationship with our students is so important. It is one of our biggest challenges.

Through the disruptions, especially the fear of school violence, Dols reminds us why we are in education: to be positive forces in the lives of young people.

Teaching is personal. It is not an exercise in which one person (the teacher) stands in front of the 35 other people (the students) and pontificates for 55 minutes. I am a social studies teacher. I love history, government, and geography, but that is not why I teach. I teach because I want to change kids' lives for the better. I want to be a force of positivity in their lives. In order to do that I must get to know them and allow them to get to know me. I don't build walls; I tear them down. It would be a fallacy to say that the safety of my kids is a high priority in my day-to-day life as a classroom teacher. It is there, however. Their safety is tied directly to my knowledge of who they are as individuals and who they are collectively. . . . The focus of our educational system should always be the edification and growth of the students we have the honor and privilege to teach. In many respects we have lost sight of that simplistic vision of education. It is my daily pursuit of connections to my students that I use as a tool to change the lives and impact the futures of my students. They are the reason I am there.

Note the dominant similar strand between Grawer and Dols: the need to foster positive relationships in the lives of young people. Regardless of the century or the generation, young people need guides in their lives to show them the way. In today's world, we must know them to understand them—and continue working to keep them safe.

Tips for Maintaining Student Safety in an Age of Disruptions

⚡ **Monitor student social media.**

It used to be angry students could only share their feelings, insults, or threats if they were speaking with someone in person or on a telephone landline. Now social media wars erupt on the weekends. Social media gives young people a 24/7 opportunity to impulsively broadcast their thoughts—without thinking of the consequences. Know what they are sharing.

⚡ **More than ever, know your students.**

Be aware of what is normal and abnormal for your students. Don't build walls; tear them down.

⚡ **Teachers teach; administrators guard the doors.**

Teachers must be free to focus on teaching; yet they must be aware of student safety issues and always keep those issues in the backs of their minds. Administrators have a larger view of what is happening in the school and neighborhood and must provide leadership and ideas for student safety.

⚡ **Local law enforcement officers are essential partners.**

We used to call the police into schools only when we had problems; now they play critical roles in relationships with students, provide information on what is happening in the neighborhood, and assist school leaders in gaining access to additional resources.

⚡ **Cope, adjust, and transform.**

The days of the strong leader working independently to eliminate problems are gone. Leading schools through disruptions requires vision and a team effort. School leaders must work with all parties to effectively deal with disruptive events in their early stages, to reflect on them in the following weeks and months, and to build awareness that future disruptive events are a probability.

Chapter 3 Scenarios for Applying the CAT Strategy

Scenario 1: The mother of a student accuses another student of bullying her daughter through social media. One night the mother begins to send the other student hateful messages. That student's mother sees them and begins to respond online in the same manner. The next morning both mothers go to the school to seek help from the administration. They happen to arrive at the same time, see each other in the outer office, and begin to argue loudly and physically threaten each other. The principal, who had been in a classroom, arrives and tries to keep them apart, but the two mothers begin to physically fight. An assistant principal puts the school in lockdown as the principal immediately calls for the school resource officer and works with the officer to pull the parents apart. Other police officers arrive. The mothers are placed under arrest, they are removed from the building, and the lockdown is ended.

Cope: The principal checks to see everyone in the office is okay, reassures them that calm has been restored to the building, and quickly sends an e-mail to the staff telling them what happened. The principal then consults with the two daughters to try to resolve the situation. The principal tries to be visible in the halls and classrooms that day to reassure anxious students and staff.

Adjust: In the days after the event, the principal meets with the staff to review security procedures, especially for when visitors become violent. The principal adds a security camera in the office area and works with the administrative team and school resource officer to brainstorm ways to respond even more quickly to future events.

Transform: In the months following the event, the principal continues to proactively work with students to educate them on cyberbullying, ways to report it, and peaceful ways to cope with it. The principal does the same work with parent groups. The principal reminds the staff they are now in an age where insults and threats that are posted online one night can result in violence the next day and all staff members must continue to work with students to resolve issues and create peaceful avenues of expression. The principal continues to tell them this is a part of their jobs in educating 21st century students.

Scenario 2: An Internet video about people dressed as clowns attacking a school has gone viral. A principal begins to get phone calls from concerned parents after their children tell them a person dressed as a clown has been seen in some woods directly behind the school. When the principal checks with the police about the rumor, the principal is told that a person dressed as a clown was seen in some woods in another part of town but not near the school. The person was waiving a knife at people in passing cars as a joke and was arrested for inducing a panic.

Cope: In the days after the arrest, the principal uses social media and e-mail to assure students, parents, and staff that the school is safe and an arrest of someone committing a prank has been made on the other side of town. The principal asks the staff to keep an eye on the woods behind the school in case someone else attempts to pull a similar prank or do something dangerous. The principal assures the students, parents, and staff that school personnel are on heightened security.

Adjust: In the weeks after the incident, the principal works with students to help them understand that viral videos might create issues in a school but they should remain calm and feel free to communicate with school personnel if they hear of any threats or are feeling concerned.

Transform: In the months after the clown viral video craze has subsided, the principal has the staff reflect on the power of the Internet to affect young people. The principal tells them the next viral video could deeply impact students in their school, even if the video was made in another state or even another country. The principal and the staff decide to be more proactive in the future when the next viral video appears that involves a school threat; instead of hoping the video won't affect them, they will reach out to students and parents immediately when they hear of the video so they can discuss its contents and what everyone can do to promote school safety.

ACTIVITIES TO CREATE A SAFER SCHOOL IN THE 21ST CENTURY

1. List the ways you monitor what is happening in your student population.

   - Do you have formal leaders (students who hold official leadership positions within your school) whom you ask to assist you?

   - Do you have informal leaders (students who don't hold official leadership positions within your school but are plugged into what is happening in the halls and in the neighborhood) whom you ask to assist you?

   - Do you have an established student/staff safety committee to guide you?

   - Do you or other staff members help monitor student social media?

2. List the ways law enforcement officials assist you in maintaining a safe environment.

   - Do you have key officers to whom you can turn to find out what is happening in the area?

   - Are there officers, especially school resource officers, who have positive relationships with students and can proactively work with students?

   - Are the local law enforcement agencies aware of the layout of your building? Do they ever enter your building to tour it or to drill in it?

3. List the initiatives you have to prevent bullying in your building.

   - Do you have established programs to educate students and assist them?

   - Do you have any accurate data on how much bullying is occurring?

   - If you want to learn more, are there schools within the area that have effective anti-bullying programs?

4. List the ways you are assisting students with mental health issues in your building.

   - What trends are you seeing with regard to student mental health? Do you have reliable data? Are the issues increasing? What are the stressors?

   - Is everyone in the building aware of the resources available to students?

   - How can you partner with outside agencies to provide more help for your students?

5. Apply the CAT method to an event from the past in your building.

PROMPTS FOR UNDERSTANDING	YOUR DISRUPTIVE EVENT
Describe the disruptive event that included a student safety issue.	
How did you cope with it in the days following its inception?	
How did you adjust your practices or policies in the weeks after the event?	
How did you transform your philosophy or your staff's philosophy to better deal with future safety events?	
Looking back, what went well?	
What could have gone better?	
Is there anything else you or your staff learned by going through the event?	
Do you think you and your staff are better prepared to deal with future safety disruptions and to use them to your advantage?	

Technology

New Opportunities and New Challenges

Tech = good.

—Derek McCoy, Principal

A merican school disruptions used to be American made. Whatever happened in American society could be seen happening in our schools. Generation gaps, civil rights issues, violence, cultural trends ranging from attitudes to dress—if they popped up in America, then they worked their way into the culture and operations of American schools. While we still confront a vast array of national disruptions, globalization has added a new dimension: Global barriers are dropping, and some of the waves of American school change might be starting overseas instead of in Washington, D.C.

This is especially true of technology disruptions. In the past, the latest projectors, copiers, and other technology that changed American education were designed and made in America, but this is no longer the case. Ideas for new software might begin in Silicon Valley or Austin, but they could be brought to fruition by engineers located in Seattle or Charlotte who are working with colleagues in Tokyo and Bonn. The tablets in our schools might be made in China or India and shipped across the ocean on massive freighters. And new apps? They can come from almost anywhere. A safe rule for school leaders to remember is this: If new technology and social media sites are created anywhere in the world, then it's only a matter of time before their impact is felt in American society—and then in our schools.

We have to be ready for them. Instead of fearing change brought about by technology or being overwhelmed by social media, school leaders need to see the latest mind-boggling devices or advances in software and social media as

- symbols of an accelerating world,

- reminders that graduates must be able to cope with a world constantly being redesigned, and

- opportunities for improving education and communication.

Technology disruptions have opened incredible new avenues for teaching and learning. When used inappropriately in a school, technology is a distraction—but when used appropriately, it is the greatest change agent in education.

THE IMPACT OF TECHNOLOGY

Consider the trail of education disruptions that have been brought about because of technology. The Internet continues to be built out, which has led to cloud development, which has led to online learning, which has led to 24/7 education opportunities. Processing speed has accelerated dramatically, which has led to a greater variety of devices, which has led to lower prices, which has led to an increase of technology use in our schools.

Suddenly, school is wherever there's an Internet connection; learning is anyplace students can access the cloud on personal computers, tablets, or smartphones. What was memorized in the past can now be brought up on a screen in a few seconds, often with accompanying video, which raises incredible questions about curriculum, instruction, and assessment in 21st century schools. Technology's created more transparency for parents to access grades online and for citizens to see how their tax dollars are being spent. Social media has connected students, parents, and teachers. There are no secrets; everything that happens in a school can be broadcast to the world and dissected on Twitter. We now have new terms like *cybersecurity* and *cyberbullying*—and evolving school-wide safety issues to go with them. With technology, the world—with all its beauty and foibles—is now at the fingertips of our students.

And we're starting to tap into the power of technology in schools. While American schools remain trapped for various reasons in a 20th century model, pockets of progressive practices are beginning to form. A few school leaders are taking bold steps to push, pull, and cajole their schools to the forefront of change; they have recognized the disruption and have jumped into the middle of it to learn more.

FOUR KEY POINTS FOR LEADERS ABOUT TECHNOLOGY DISRUPTIONS

One of these progressive leaders is Angie Adrean, the principal of Worthington Kilbourne High School, in a suburb of Columbus, Ohio. In 2016, she was named the Ohio High School Principal of the Year. She knows the 20th century principal responsibilities—like forming relationships, maintaining high academic standards, and completing the daily tasks of leading a 1,600-student high school—are still huge parts of her job. But she also has her mind turned to the future—and she recognizes the role technology plays in the personal lives of her students and the role it must play in school redesign. When asked what educators need to do with technology in this age of disruption, she says emphatically, "EMBRACE IT!"

Here are four key points Adrean has used to help her staff embrace technology and lead her school to the front of the technology evolution.

Angie Adrean, Principal
Worthington Kilbourne High School
Columbus, Ohio

Four Key Points for Leading a School to Embrace the Technology Revolution

1. Let students use technology to tap into the power of "What if . . . ?"

2. Allow technology to change the role of the teacher.

3. Model the ways to use technology disruptions when training educators.

4. Be proactive in helping students manage their social media.

Point 1: Let Students Use Technology to Tap Into the Power of "What If . . . ?"

At the core of Adrean's philosophy is the belief that we must allow students to use technology to unwrap the secrets of the world. She knows technology puts the awe in learning.

Change is fast-paced in education, but our school response to these changes is not. We want a relevant environment for our students, and that relevancy is not gained by teaching our students the way we were taught. If schools do not address the purpose of technology in learning, our students will disconnect when they enter the school and reconnect as they exit. We have to embrace this fast-paced change and open the doors to the ideas of our students. We must model and embed the growth mindset practice of Carol Dweck and teach this to our students. Simply conforming to our current practices is not enough, we have to provide multiple platforms for our students to be brave and disrupt the status quo. I want our teachers and our students to confidently say, "What if?" versus "Yeah, but . . . !"

Adrean doesn't want to just manage technology; she wants to unleash her students' minds by getting them to ask, "What if . . . ?" Isn't this one of the greatest questions students can ask? She wants her school to become an extension of what students do in their private lives and not a place where they just use pens, pencils, paper, and textbooks to explore the world.

But a key point is she is brave enough to embrace the unknown. While many educators fear losing control, she openly encourages her students to use technology to upset the status quo. She knows education is not memorizing facts anymore; in her school she's promoting exploration and application. She wants her students online hunting for information. When students are allowed to process and think for themselves, educators have less control over student views; the students might not give the answers educators are expecting. Some educators try to control the box in which their students learn, but Adrean has taken a different approach: Her students live outside the box, and she doesn't want to force them back into it.

She understands technology disruptions haven't just changed teaching and learning; they've disrupted how we should view education. We can't measure student success only through grades anymore, nor can we seek the set answers of the past. Learning at the K–12 level must be centered on open-ended questions for which there are no clear answers, which means K–12 learning in this century will be messy. Students must truly be our partners in charting the path forward, a path that will evolve as society and the global economy shifts. Adrean and her students and staff might not know what's waiting around the next bend, but they are committed to approaching it together.

Point 2: Allow Technology to Change the Role of the Teacher

Another point Adrean stresses is one of the most difficult concepts for many educators to grasp: Technology allows the teacher to become a facilitator of knowledge acquisition. For years, educators have said teachers must transition a significant part of their time from using too much direct instruction to allowing students to have more control over their learning, but it's a difficult goal to achieve. Technology can be a vehicle for allowing this to happen; it can disrupt teaching in a positive way.

When technology supports the learning like it should in today's classroom, the role of the teacher changes. It's wonderful to see the teacher

(Continued)

(Continued)

transform from the sole distributer of information to a facilitator. When I reflect on learning when I was in school, it seemed that the quieter the teacher kept the class, the more we were learning. At least that was the myth. Technology has allowed teachers to personalize learning for all students. Technology promotes student choice. Technology provides a different classroom structure for the teachers. The teacher is now available to reflect with students in small group settings while providing immediate, constructive feedback for all. Today's learners started learning with technology in their hands and will continue to do so. This learning tool is valued by our students, and when teachers take the time to plan for the integration of technology, it naturally adds value to the learning standards and motivates them to discover more.

Technology supports a student-centered classroom. While I often hear that technology is taking away social skills for our children, I believe the opposite. Technology promotes collaboration and allows for students to control their learning. In a collaborative, technology-friendly classroom, desks are not in rows facing the teacher at the front of the classroom. The teacher is a participant, guiding the lesson and allowing for students to research and dig deeper into the content with a valuable resource at their fingertips.

Technology also provides us with the capability of creating assessments that allow students to utilize reflection and synthesis when sharing their knowledge and understanding. Today's learner requires IMMEDIATE feedback, and technology provides this for all students.

She brings up key aspects of technology when it is employed successfully in the classroom:

- It promotes student choice and personalized learning.
- It creates a student-centered classroom and promotes collaboration.
- It helps the teacher become a participant.
- It allows for immediate feedback from the teacher and from peers.

Technology permits learning to take place 24/7 and opens the door for some deep discussions on best practices; it provides opportunities to move forward—and sometimes to fall forward when things don't go as planned.

School leaders must prepare students to thrive in the 21st century by encouraging them to take more control of their learning. For today's graduates to succeed in a global economy, they will have to be decision makers, self-motivated, and risk takers. These are not traits that suddenly appear on graduation day; they must be a part of K–12 education, and the technology disruptions make them necessary school skills.

Point 3: Model the Ways to Use Technology Disruptions When Training Educators

The transition to 21st century teaching includes rethinking how we use technology disruptions in professional development. Adrean recognizes the need to show her staff how she, too, is using technology in their training.

Technology has certainly changed the structure of our staff meetings over the years. Twenty-five years ago when I began my work as an art teacher, staff meetings were my nemesis. I learned rather quickly that to make the best use of that hour of my time I needed to plan ahead and be sure to bring work with me. Either that or utilize the time to make my next grocery list. Okay, maybe it wasn't that bad, but it was certainly not a collaborative, productive time for us. The way we as first-year teachers start teaching like we were taught, I also conducted my first staff meeting using those traditional techniques.

Fortunately, my staff meetings today take on a different look. Our teachers are structured in teacher-based teams (TBTs), and much of our staff meeting time is focused on this work. Google Classroom is our platform for all TBTs, and the five-step process is documented by one member of the TBT throughout the school year. We also have a Building Leadership Team that monitors the work of our TBT and provides ongoing feedback throughout the school year.

My hope is that our teachers and staff enter each staff meeting with a sense of purpose and leave with a sense of accomplishment. I can share dates and other important information in an e-mail or a weekly update. Our teachers desire to learn as do our students, and I must provide them the time necessary to help them collaborate with others so that they can continue to learn and grow.

Most teachers allow cell phones to be present in the classroom but at times will ask students to put them away if they are not a part of the

(Continued)

(Continued)

lesson. I do see cell phones becoming somewhat of an addition to our students, but in the same breath, I also see this addiction with some of our adults. It's not just students. . . . I try to model ways to use the cell phone in class during our staff meetings, like with QR readers, Quizlet, Twitter, Backchannel, Voxer, Flipboard, Remind, GroupMe, and so on.

The line is blurring between teaching educators and teaching students. Many of the same training rules apply today for professional development:

- The topic must be relevant.
- Teachers must be allowed to collaborate.
- The initiatives must be embedded and ongoing.
- The assessment should be nonthreatening and formative.
- The teachers must be partners in the design and implementation.
- Technology must be integrated throughout the various initiatives, from teacher research to online collaboration opportunities.

A good rule for leaders who design professional development is to treat the students the way they would treat the adults—and as strange as it sounds, to treat the adults the way you treat the students. Technology disruptions have changed expectations for everyone. It's a swipe-and-go society; people of all ages want choice and control in their learning.

Point 4: Be Proactive in Helping Students Manage Their Social Media

Technology disruptions can be divided into two categories: the advances that are transforming teaching and learning—and social media that is broadcasting everything to the world. When social media entered our students' lives (and of course, entered our schools), some students began to post videos of hallway fights, organize protests, and publish harmful posts about other students. For many school leaders, their introduction to social media led to negative, career-changing events; they suddenly found themselves confronting a new, complicated issue without fully understanding how or why it was all happening. It's no surprise that many of them wish they had never heard of Twitter, YouTube, or Facebook.

However, in recent years more school leaders have begun to understand the importance of helping students appropriately manage their social media posts and to understand how to use social media to their schools' advantage. Like most administrators, Adrean has managed a wide range of cell phone and social media issues—and she has developed an adaptive mindset in approaching them.

It is truly difficult for me to remember what learning was like in schools without social media as a resource. I chuckle when I think about how much we focused on ensuring that students did not possess or even utilize a cell phone (back then, a flip phone). It makes me nauseous to think about the hours we spent on punitive discipline for possession or use . . . the paperwork, the phone calls home, the searches—ridiculous. While I say it is difficult for me to remember, it was only 5 years ago when I started a new position as a high school principal, and upon entering the building, I immediately noticed signs stating NO CELL PHONE ZONE. Those were the first signs I removed as the new principal. While I was confident in my own belief in the importance of technology and social media in learning, I knew that it might not be the smartest thing for me to tackle as a new high school principal. While the students might appreciate the change, the staff and teachers might have a different perspective. :-) I had to make sure that I approached these changes using a voice of reason while valuing the diverse perspectives of our teachers and staff. I learned that just because I have a strong belief in an educational practice, it does not mean everyone else does.

Like any other learning resource, we have to help our students discover the most appropriate avenues to learn and grow through the use of technology. We can expect them to make mistakes and at times allow their curiosity to lead them down an inappropriate path. This is not all bad if you are confident enough in yourself to allow the student to teach you. If the student takes ownership of this not-so-appropriate path, let them tell you why it's not appropriate or why their actions are not conducive to a safe school environment. You can't get too worked up; do you really believe they have not seen worse?

(Continued)

(Continued)

Superintendents and principals must transition from 20th century managers to 21st century leaders. Their mindsets must move from punishing students for their cell phone use to encouraging them to employ technology. Effective school leaders don't always resolve disruptive social media events by implementing new student discipline policies; they often teach students through proactive steps that guide them to make better choices.

One of the toughest aspects of today's leadership involves leading through an era of change while some team members have not yet bought into the vision—or perhaps are still using a 20th century mindset. School leaders must nurture the thinking and practices of teachers moving to the future and try to leave room for those who have not yet evolved.

But the school must keep moving. Adrean, who has successfully bridged the gap between centuries, has this motto: "Train the best; drag the rest!"

Coping, Adjusting, and Transforming With Social Media

Disruptive events involving social media often arise suddenly. One minute it's quiet, and the next minute they are bursting over the school like fireworks on the Fourth of July. They consume time and energy, and there's often a lot to clean up afterward. School leaders shouldn't be surprised when these disruptions occur; they need to have a proactive CAT (cope, adjust, and transform) process in place for helping their students, staff, and community deal with these events and treat them as learning opportunities.

Here's an example of the first steps Adrean took when a disruptive event in social media entered her school.

During my first year as a high school principal, we experienced an inappropriate, hurtful Twitter feed titled "CONFESSIONS." Negative comments were being made about individuals associated with our school community: students, teachers, staff, parents, and community members. Upon much investigation, I discovered that this same feed was active in several area high schools.

I paused . . . and reached out to several of my mentors and coworkers. I spoke with a few parents and students to get their thoughts and soon after drafted a parent letter asking for their help and assistance.

I shared brief background information and asked them to help me talk with their child. I scripted what I had planned to share so that our message was consistent. EVERY parent supported our work, because it was done together. This is when Dr. Tim Conrad (a TWHS [Thomas Worthington High School] parent) read my e-mail and reached out to me, and I accepted his help.

In the weeks after she began to cope with "CONFESSIONS," Adrean adjusted her practices by involving a committee of students who could lay the groundwork for future initiatives.

I knew I was not going to "fix" this without involvement of several of our student leaders, so I immediately reached out to our Principal's Advisory Council. I started this leadership council in the summer prior to the opening of school during my first year. It is made up of five diverse student leaders from each grade level. These students help me gauge the heartbeat of our building. Their voice is of utmost importance to the culture/climate success of our high school. They keep me grounded in my work as a high school principal.

Adrean has transformed her mindset around social media and implemented long-term guiding points and practices that are ongoing and effective.

Student ownership is the method that has worked for us. Thanks to Dr. Tim Conrad and Officer Don Stanko, authors of Digital Danger: If You Think Your Child Is Safe Online, Think Again, *we are on the right track with a student-leader/train-the-trainer model regarding social media safety. . . . Each year, I work with 25 student leaders from my Principal's Advisory Council. We have increased their knowledge in social media and they now work with middle school and elementary students across the district. We have also presented to local community organizations and at the OASSA Fall Conference.*

For the past 3 years, our Principal's Advisory Council has brought awareness to the importance of a "digital footprint." We have conducted parent book talks with our high school parents and "Where do you draw the line?" trainings with our middle and elementary schools . . . all led by our WKHS students.

(Continued)

(Continued)

If you want technology to be a learning tool, allow the students to help you create the expectations. They know what is right and wrong, and if you have a trusting relationship with them, they'll tell you more than you may want to know. :-)

Angie Adrean: Social Media Tips for Students

- *Do not correspond with people you have not met or meet anyone in person whom you have talked with online.*

- *Be open with your parents about your Internet use. Parents, please monitor your child's Internet use.*

- *Once you post, you can't take it back. . . . The Internet is not forgiving. "Delete doesn't mean delete." When I am talking with students, they will say this before I can, because they have heard me say it so much.*

- *We also talk a lot about the impression they give to others through social media, specifically future employers and colleges/universities.*

Angie Adrean: Social Media Tips for Staff

- *Build a culture where students start to correct one another.*

- *Be knowledgeable of social media—use it!*

- *Use it to highlight your school's success. If you don't brand your school, no one else will.*

- *Let kids know you care.*

- *Let them know how proud you are of them. I use the hashtag #ProudPrincipal on lots of my posts. At graduation, the students referred to this by saying #ProudStudents in their speech.*

- *I can't stress how important it is for leaders to know what apps the students are using. I have been known to sit at students' lunch tables with the goal of having them teach me how to use a new app. We have to put our pride aside and collaborate with the students to better understand their interests and learning needs.*

Students are critical partners when implementing social media best practices. School leaders should get student input when educating students about social media, set guidelines to help students make ethical and safe choices, and use social media in their schools to help create a culture of trust. School leaders must understand the power of this new tool to help brand a school as a positive place where students are supported and learning is valued. And just as important, they must be practitioners to understand what the students are doing online and how technology disruptions are shaping their world.

FROM MYSPACE TO PERSONAL DEVICES AND THE CLOUD

Jason Markey is an innovative high school principal at East Leyden High School in Franklin Park, Illinois. He, too, has seen the rapid changes—both good and bad—technology has brought to education in the classroom and outside the school.

Stories From Exceptional Educational Leaders

Jason Markey, Principal
East Leyden High School
Franklin Park, Illinois

At the beginning of my career the central hub of technology in the classroom was a TV and an overhead projector. The only Internet connection was in the department office down the hall and a few computers in the library that were connected to the Internet. During my last few years teaching before moving to administration, I witnessed the onset of social media with Myspace. A colleague and I quickly tried to understand the energy of connecting students this way and started to use a closed social network to have our students join students from different schools in discussions and collaboration. Finally, as a high school principal the past 5 years, I've seen our school give every student a device that is driven by the Internet, actually having its entire operating system delivered over the web! This has allowed technology to become fuller and more seamlessly

(Continued)

(Continued)

integrated into a student's education, providing greater opportunity for authentic and student-centered learning.

Student Input and Digital Citizenship

Markey was one of the first principals to tap into the positive power of social media, and in doing so he turned to the experts for advice: his students.

Social media has moved out of the shadows of the early days of Myspace and then Facebook to the world of school hashtags and filters on Twitter and Snapchat. I believe more and more schools see leveraging social media as not only full of positive potential for their school but also as a responsibility to allow students to engage in the digital world and truly learn what digital citizenship means in our current context. At Leyden we were very quick to make this move during my first year as principal when a few students demonstrated concern over the types of things they saw other students saying on Twitter. The students were convinced that our school could do better, and we brainstormed together the idea of starting a school hashtag, #leydenpride, that would go on to become the collective voice of our school. This demonstrated to all of our students a few important things: both that we valued every student's voice and that we trusted them to own the conversation. The fact that we established a hashtag meant that anyone could contribute and no one controlled the conversations. I am constantly impressed by how our students will go above and beyond our expectations, and even on the occasion when something inappropriate is posted, it offers an authentic opportunity to have a conversation with a student about digital citizenship.

When Markey encounters issues, he strives to take a positive approach to resolving them.

We have attempted to take a restorative approach to any issues that have arisen with the use of technology. We certainly strive to make sure the individual recognizes what the issue is, but we also want to ensure that they understand that they are a valued member of our community and we want to make sure they understand that we value them and want them to live up to the standards we have set. We think it's important to address the behavior, not the method of communicating, so we have largely worked within our existing policies. I believe our staff recognizes that as a school we are more aware and proactive regarding social media than many schools, allowing our students to have our school's support as they navigate our constantly shifting digital landscape.

Markey embodies a trait that is essential for 21st century school leadership: the ability to see the positive aspects of change and not just the challenges change creates. Every disruption in history has created challenges; yet they are the stitching that leads to better lives.

And to a better education for young people.

My hope is that technology will be leveraged to further connect our students with the global community and make authentic contributions through their education. We see this more and more in our individual schools, but the more we can connect our students across school district boundaries, it will continue to strengthen our society as these students will naturally build empathy for one another. School leaders should connect and model the same connectedness we wish to see in our students by embracing and modeling the use of technology. I consistently try to retweet our students and teachers, share their learning with colleagues in other schools, and look for intersections of collaboration that are possible to bring back to our students.

THE DIFFICULTY OF CHANGE

Derek McCoy is the acclaimed principal of West Rowan Middle School in Salisbury, North Carolina. He began his career in the past century as a middle school remedial reading teacher in Georgia, but he saw the value of the technology wave that was entering education. He became certified as an Apple Classroom of Tomorrow teacher, and he received a Georgia technology certification known as InTech. He began training other teachers and has learned a great deal about the challenges and benefits of helping educators move from textbooks to technology.

Derek McCoy, Principal

West Rowan Middle School

Salisbury, North Carolina

Change is hard, always has been, doesn't matter the context or the year. Some of the conversations I had then are the same as now.

One of the biggest things I had to go through was deprogramming myself from my own K–16 learning experiences. I wanted to bring them to my classroom. That immediately proved problematic. And as an alternative certified teacher, it was more difficult. I see the same in teachers today. Despite teacher ed training, they bring their thoughts of what a classroom should be, and it's often based on their own K–16 experiences. It is work deprogramming these beliefs.

McCoy is a huge advocate for getting devices into the hands of young people.

Cell phones first came in my purview in schools when I was an administrator 2002–2004. It wasn't just talk about banning them; it was fear talk from adults. There was a video made about how cell phone calls can trigger bombs. It was scary to see and put us on a mission to find cell phones and suspend kids for "jeopardizing lives."

The terror minimized over the years [thanks to coaching from great principals], but the fear/need to ban was still there. It wasn't until I became a connected educator that that changed, especially hearing success stories in other schools.

Now I am a proponent of BYOD [bring your own device] policies. My last two schools, I have brought BYOD policies to bear. At Spring Lake Middle, my previous school—urban, Title 1, high needs—we implemented a BYOD policy with great success. Students would bring in devices often damaged badly or with no service just so they could listen to music while they worked. Teachers there worked hard at teaching responsible behavior. It changed how kids worked. At my current school, the summer I got hired, I walked through halls and took down signs that showed cells banned. I modeled BYOD strategies by establishing when to get connected during meetings and when not to. It is about teaching behaviors and expectations—not focusing on hypotheticals.

Embrace devices. I wrote a blog post about empowerment versus engagement in using student devices to help not just engage kids but design great work to have them dive deep. If they are immersed in great work, who cares if they listen to music on their own devices? When we think of them as distractions, we lose sight of potential. We need to build a vision of what learning can look like with personal technology and build talks, trainings, and school cultures to that effect.

McCoy makes an important point about digital tools: We have to use the right ones to accomplish certain tasks.

It used to be about learning any and all tools that came in front of me. In fact, I do enjoy it. Learning and sharing digital tools was an early passion of mine. But now it is about the work we need to do. We look at the goal we are trying to accomplish, the vision set ahead of us, and then we think of tools to use. Sometimes, I will reach out to my PLN [personal learning network] to ask if there is a better tool to accomplish what we need. We make it about the goal at the end—not the flash of the tool.

We will start asking better questions about technology (in the future). I think most tools are for independent learning. Some of the better ones have adaptive tech; questions can get easier or harder based on input. This is still independent. Once tech gets personalized, it will incorporate adaptive research opportunities, giving kids the chance to explore something they are passionate about AND giving some form of guidance/facilitation. AI is growing and will be made more mainstream.

And finally, McCoy gives us this simple mantra to guide us: *Tech = good.*

Tips for Leading Schools in an Age of Technology Disruptions

⚡ Technology is a disruption that has brought fear to some educators; instead, it should be used to tap into the power of 21st century minds.

⚡ Move from low levels of knowledge and application to allowing students to ask "what if" questions and seek answers.

⚡ More than ever, teachers want to be participants in their professional learning, not just passive listeners in seminars. Involve them; let them use technology in training. Model best practices so technology is embedded in the teaching and training is available to them on a 24/7 basis.

⚡ Social media is a powerful tool—or weapon—in the hands of young people. Help students understand the ethical uses of social media and how to use it in a constructive manner.

⚡ Use the right tool for the task.

⚡ Students are no longer silent participants; ask them to be your partners in using educational technology and social media. And try to let them lead.

Chapter 4 Scenarios for Applying the CAT Strategy

Scenario 1: A female student sends some inappropriate photos to a male student. In some photos she is wearing only her underwear, and in others she is topless. The male student shares the photos online with his friends, who share the photos with their friends. All this occurs outside of school hours. Within a few days many students in the school have seen the photos. The girl becomes the subject of jokes and harassing remarks in the school, and her parents approach the principal asking for help.

Cope: In the days after the principal hears of the issue, the principal talks with the girl, gets her help through the guidance office, and quietly speaks with her teachers so they can also help her. The male student is questioned, and the police are brought in to determine if the students distributed photos that could be considered pornographic. The principal determines if any of the students violated school policies and if they should be punished.

Adjust: In the weeks after the event, the principal checks in with the girl to see how she is doing, and the principal also checks on her progress by speaking with her teachers and her parents. The principal has a meeting of a student-led advisory group. When the subject of photo sharing is broached by a student, the principal is ready with some helpful tips the students can quietly and tactfully share with other students to prevent it from happening again or to help others in the same situation. The principal also gives advice on what to do when students receive inappropriate material (show it to a trusted adult and then be prepared to delete it).

Transform: In the months after the photo-sharing event, the principal continues to work with student groups and staff to make them aware of digital safety guidelines that include what to share and what not to share. The principal and staff members decide to increase their efforts to educate the students on digital ethics and digital safety. They incorporate safety videos, what-if scenarios for students, and guest speakers from the police department.

Scenario 2: An English teacher has been using a free online website to support literature activities in class. The teacher creates a teacher account, and the students create student accounts. The teacher gives a few assignments over the course of a 2-month period in which the students go online to answer homework questions that are then graded by the teacher. However, some students learn that because the website is free and open to

(Continued)

(Continued)

anyone, they can go into the site, pretend to be a teacher, and open a teacher account, which gives them answers to the homework questions. To create the teacher accounts they affirm they are teachers and create fictional answers to questions about the types of schools in which they teach and the technology they use in the classroom. Eventually, a student feels guilty about cheating and tells the teacher what is occurring, and the teacher informs the principal.

Cope: In the days after the teacher and principal hear of the event, they talk to numerous students who admit to cheating. The principal and teacher decide on an appropriate punishment, and they try to make the discipline a teachable event for the students. The principal also has lengthy conversations with the parents of the students to inform them of what has occurred, the punishment involved, and lessons they can reinforce with the students.

Adjust: In the weeks after the event, the principal works with students in various groups to help them understand that just because something is available and free on the Internet doesn't make it right to use or download it. This is a hard lesson for Gen Z students, who grew up with the Internet and access to a wide variety of sites. The principal also warns all teachers that if they are using free, openly accessible sites, they are subject to security breaches.

Transform: In the months after the event, the principal and staff create internal guidelines for using free sites: (1) The sites can be used to augment instruction but not for graded work, (2) teachers should take the opportunity to discuss digital ethics to students when they first start using the sites, (3) and the teachers and students need to continue to discuss the appropriate way to use the sites in the months after they are introduced so the ideas will be reinforced in student behavior. The principal also uses the conversation with teachers as an opportunity to share Gen Z's view of the Internet and how teachers can effectively use the Internet to match Gen Z's learning style.

Put the Awe in Education

1. List the ways you or some educators with whom you work are allowing students to use technology to do more than just complete their assignments—to explore their world and to develop a sense of awe in learning.

2. Think of a recent circumstance in which a student completed a creative project using technology. What did the teacher do to foster it? Why was the student successful? Did you do anything afterward to reinforce the teacher's or student's effort and to help replicate it in other classrooms?

3. List the names of the teachers in your building who you know are leading the way in fostering creativity through technology and can assist you in planning and implementation of teacher training. List other ways they can help you and create a timeline to chart your progress.

Use Technology to Move From Control to Facilitation

Consider how you as a leader urge teachers to use technology to promote creativity, assessment, and individuality in the classroom.

4. Fostering creativity

   Do you urge teachers to guide all parts of the lesson, including how students will use technology, or do you urge teachers to have clear learning targets that will allow students freedom in how they can use technology?

5. Flexible assessment

   Do you urge teachers to have firm grading guidelines in place, or do you urge teachers to be flexible to allow for student creativity?

(Continued)

(Continued)

6. Promoting individuality

   Do you urge teachers to get students through the curriculum in the same way, or do you actively encourage them to use technology to allow students more freedom in approaching the curriculum?

7. Promoting student leadership

   Can you find ways to allow students to lead the staff when implementing technology? Can you form a student committee to assist teachers, or are there key students who can be available to help with implementation?

Use Technology in Professional Development

8. Do you model the traits you'd like to see in classrooms as you create professional development by making technology an essential part of the training?

9. Do you provide objectives and assistance but allow teachers freedom to creatively use technology to implement units, assessments, and teaching methods?

10. Since adults are like young people and learn at different speeds, do you have flexible timelines for educators to complete professional development projects?

11. Do you have a system or method in place that encourages educators to share new apps, programs, and methods with their peers?

12. Are your training activities available online 24/7 to allow educators to access them when it is convenient for them?

13. What else can you do to improve or reinforce your best practices with using technology in professional development?

Help Students and Staff Use Technology and Social Media Ethically

14. What do you do to promote the ethical use of technology and social media among students and staff?

15. Do you have published guidelines in place?

16. Do you have a group of students and staff members who assist you in forming technology and social media guidelines, setting initiatives, and dealing with issues?

17. How do you involve parents?

18. How do you communicate with other school leaders to share information?

19. Do you have a network of outside resources such as police officers and other experts to assist you?

20. Do you have access to a list of books, blogs, and websites to which you can refer when seeking information or sharing it with others?

Cope, Adjust, and Transform With Technology Disruptions

Use the following chart to reflect on a technology disruptive event in your school and what you did to cope, adjust, and transform with it. Read the prompts on the left and fill in the boxes on the right. Feel free to work through this process with multiple disruptive events to look for patterns and clues for future success.

PROMPTS FOR UNDERSTANDING	YOUR DISRUPTIVE EVENT
Describe the disruptive event involving technology.	
How did you cope with it in the days following its inception?	
How did you adjust your practices or policies in the weeks after the event?	
How did you transform your philosophy or your staff's philosophy to better deal with future technology disruptive events?	

(Continued)

(Continued)

PROMPTS FOR UNDERSTANDING	YOUR DISRUPTIVE EVENT
Looking back, what went well?	
What could have gone better?	
Is there anything else you or your staff learned by going through the event?	
Do you think you and your staff are better prepared to deal with future technology disruptions and to use them to your advantage?	

Education Reforms

Searching for the Freedom to Lead and the Freedom to Teach

Because education is continually receiving blows in the form of new initiatives and/or mandates, the people doing the job can't gain a foothold. Thus, we really don't know what target to aim for.

—Dr. Jay R. Dostal, Principal

There is a pervasive feeling of helplessness in the face of school reform efforts. Teachers are losing control over the profession they hold so dear. We feel as if we have to fight tooth and nail to maintain a focus on development of the whole-child.

—Krista Taylor, Teacher

The new education reform initiatives just keep coming. And our educators keep shifting their efforts to keep up.

American educators know the acronyms NCLB, RTT, and ESSA. Combine them with acronyms for state testing and you have a complete alphabet soup of education reform. We have curriculum standards, massive amounts of testing, benchmarking, growth measures, and labels. Teaching and learning, for better or worse, wasn't always this complicated.

Up until the early 1980s the local school board, through the local teachers and principals, guided the content and instruction in schools. The board set the standard for excellence. But as Americans saw the rise of global competition in the 1980s, the public began to blame schools for the jobs disappearing overseas. *A Nation at Risk* in 1983 ushered in standardized testing in most states. For the next 18 years the standardized tests became increasingly more pervasive in schools, and the standards became broader and more complex; schools were placed in accountability systems with district-wide report cards.

Then the federal government got into the act in 2001 with No Child Left Behind, which expanded the accountability, and then Race to the Top and the Common Core came along, and now there's the Every Student Succeeds Act. One ingredient gets piled on top of another until the testing seems to all mix together and school leaders, teachers, students, parents, and community members are left scratching their heads trying to figure out the latest formula being used to calculate school success. In our zeal to keep up with a disrupted world, we use increasingly complicated rituals to measure young minds.

Consider just a few of the labels placed on students, teachers, and schools in various states and accountability systems: Beginning, Developing, Emerging, Developed, Highly Developed, Below Average, Average, Above Average, Skilled, Accomplished, Basic, High Achieving, Low Achieving, Safe Harbor, Exempt, School Improvement, Improving, Exemplary, Recognized, Acceptable, Unacceptable, A, B, C, D, F, Met Standard, Did Not Meet Standard, Met Alternative Standard, Excellent, Exceeds Expected Growth.

Then there's the complex Average Performance Index (or some other labeled program) used by some states to calculate how much progress students have made from year to year based on their test scores.

It's gotten so complex that many parents don't know what to make of the ratings. Some of them might try to compare schools and teachers by looking at the labels, which could change from year to year, but for many parents the labels have become incomprehensible and inconsequential; they just want their children to be safe, educated, and happy.

How should administrators cope with these waves of reform?

LIVING WITH A WARPED
SENSE OF ACCOUNTABILITY

Dr. Jay R. Dostal is the award-winning principal of Kearney High School in Kearney, Nebraska, and he is leading his school through the steady waves of education reforms. He is the son of educators, and like his parents, he has spent his life helping young people. In 2016, he was named Nebraska's Secondary Principal of the Year. He has seen disruptions through the eyes of his parents and now through the eyes of a progressive 21st century school leader. He has some ideas on what's happened—and what we can do to thrive in an age in which the education reform disruptions just keep rolling over us.

Stories From Exceptional Educational Leaders

Dr. Jay R. Dostal, Principal
Kearney High School
Kearney, Nebraska

I've been in education for 15 years, and in that time, I have seen a roller coaster of changes to the educational landscape. Growing up as a child of two teachers, I also feel that I have a pretty good timeline of events that spans even longer. I vividly remember my parents talking about outcome-based education (OBE) and thinking to myself, "This isn't such a bad concept. In fact, it makes a lot of sense that students would be taught something and at the end of the course, they should be able to achieve specific outcomes." The theory is sound, but reality sets in when elected officials, with no background in education, get involved in the process. This is what was transpiring when I entered the educational ranks as a teacher.

The authorization of No Child Left Behind took a pretty good theory and manipulated it into a ranking system that determined if schools were succeeding or failing. Setting aside my own personal opinions about applying this same type of system to our government, No Child Left Behind created a warped sense of accountability rather than focusing

(Continued)

(Continued)

on what the true goal of education should be, which is GROWTH. . . . Somewhere along the line, trust was lost in public schools and they were deemed failures. Students arrive to school every day in this country at different levels. . . . We take in students who haven't eaten in a couple of days, haven't showered, are living in shelters, are reading 3 years below grade level, or have learning/behavior disorders, and regardless of how much they grow during the time the school has them, they may still fall well below the line of acceptability that our government officials deem appropriate.

This "Ivory Tower syndrome" devalues the work that educators do on a daily basis. Instead of developing an accountability model that is focused on growth, we opted for an easier system that places far too much emphasis on one score that determines the success or failure of schools. To compound things, initiatives like Common Core and Race to the Top, and the proliferation of charter schools muddies the water even further. . . . The fact of the matter is that accountability assessments really are used for one thing—being able to rank schools. Don't believe for one second that they have anything to do with educating students and promoting growth. If that was the case, students would be able to try again if they are below proficient.

I am somewhat sheltered because I live in a state (Nebraska) that never adopted the Common Core and has legislation against charter schools because we have a very good education system in our state. More important, Nebraska values local-based decision making when it comes to how to operate schools, which is a far cry from federal initiatives that have been mandated in the past 17 years.

Dostal has experienced the challenge of keeping up with reforms. Like other administrators, he lives with their negative impact on morale, teacher retention, and the overall education of young people.

Constant change has led to a moving-target effect for educators. Because so much emphasis is placed on test scores and our country's place in international rankings, everyone is constantly looking for a silver bullet that will fix all of our woes. . . . Because education is continually receiving blows in the form of new initiatives and/or mandates, the people doing the job can't gain a foothold. Thus, we really don't know what target to aim for. What this has caused is continually taking our focus off of the issue that is most important, which is daily classroom instruction. . . .

You only need to look so far as declining enrollments in teacher education programs to see the detrimental/negative impact of initiatives that have been placed upon us. No one wants to work in a profession where the people are undervalued or devalued. We work in a business of human capital, and gains on our investments are sometimes not realized until long after students leave our schools. Building relationships with students is at the core of what we do in our profession. . . . When an educator is so worried about job security and making sure that students get a certain score on an exam, we are getting away from our core belief of developing a responsible citizen. Yes, academic achievement is VERY important, but it is only one outcome that schools focus on. . . .

The reality of the situation is that our current generation of students is falling victim to the "my generation was better than yours" paradox. What we need to realize is that we cannot and should not make gross generalizations about our current or future students based on a few outliers that make the news. Our current and future generations of students, as David Bowie so eloquently stated, "are immune to your consultations. They're quite aware of what they're going through."

While the latest education reform initiative might arrive with great fanfare, it will probably be replaced in the future by yet another reform initiative. Dostal also has three points about navigating change that are guiding him through the education reform disruptions.

We can be successful if

- teachers are satisfied with their job and the workplace in which they work;
- everyone understands the "crappy stuff" that is going to need to take place to accomplish the change and is committed to working through it together; and
- we stop trying to sell people something as the best thing to do and seek "buy-in." If it truly is the best thing to do, we shouldn't have to seek buy-in, but rather, we should seek a better understanding of why the change is necessary.

SHIELDING TEACHERS AND FOCUSING ON LEARNING

Jack Jose is the award-winning principal of Gamble High School, a public high school using Montessori principles in Cincinnati, Ohio. He has successfully led his school through impressive gains in the test scores of various education initiatives. While he is not a fan of the current standardized testing system, Jose has seen an infusion of money into his school to help raise test scores, which was used to increase training, add more technology, hire academic coaches, and improve the overall instruction. And he has witnessed the impact of testing on how the school is organized, its professional development, and how it uses many of its resources. He has seen the constantly shifting education targets as new tests were introduced, some were changed, and their accompanying accountability systems entered his school and its operations. He points to the importance of starting a new school year and not having to grapple with a new testing system.

Stories From Exceptional Educational Leaders

Jack Jose, Principal
Gamble High School
Cincinnati, Ohio

At our back-to-school staff meeting in August of 2016, I was relieved and excited to point out to my staff that this year was the first in my 7 years of leadership that NONE of these major items had changed: number of standardized tests required of our students, the grades at which students took standardized tests, how the state report card examined our results, the teacher evaluation process, required components of the teacher evaluation, or graduation requirements.

Think of it: 7 years of constant change. Educators are often told they need to be "more like business" so they can be more efficient. How many businesses could successfully adapt to 7 years of new accountability systems and keep flourishing? Yet that's what educators have done.

The world is speeding up and change cannot be stopped; schools *need* to be constantly evolving, but great school leaders around America are saying we have been placing too much emphasis on standardized testing as we have attempted to keep up with global change. Consider the collateral impact to the students at Jose's school.

There is a very narrow definition of what constitutes success and growth for students individually and as a school, and the evaluation misses key components of areas of individual student growth such as attendance, deportment, attention to detail, timeliness, ability to complete project work, and so on, and so on.

We have had to reschedule, shorten, or eliminate various programs at the school that we have to develop students' socioemotional skills due to the demands of testing. A specific example, we engage in a 2-week "intersession" each spring. Intersession is an immersive course of study, worth .25 credit, that we typically conduct during two consecutive weeks in the spring. The timing of the tests this year, when combined with AP testing, means that to provide two full weeks outside of standardized testing windows, we had to split the weeks and hold them 3 weeks apart. This obviously disrupts the immersive course of study, and weakens its power as an instructional tool.

Retesting, especially for students with disabilities, is an absolute nightmare. Many students with disabilities are allowed to have extended time when taking their tests, which means they can often only take one part of a test each day (each test is currently given in two parts), and that test could potentially take nearly the full day (if the student is allowed triple time). We had three students this fall who were facing 14 days of standardized testing FOR THE MAKE-UP TESTS ONLY. Hold that in your mind for a minute: A student with a learning disability, who did poorly on seven tests previously, could have been scheduled to take 14 consecutive days of state-mandated standardized tests above and beyond whatever instruction was happening in his classes. It ought to be a crime to do that to an adolescent.

Trying to schedule this bevy of more than a dozen tests at five different grade levels is taxing to me, my test coordinator, and my scheduler, and we devise systems to provide the needed tests and accommodations for each of our students across the school. It took more than 2 weeks of

(Continued)

(Continued)

meetings, only two of which happened during the school day, to come up with a working exam schedule. This spring we will have to create a make-up testing schedule like the first one, and then add a full testing schedule for this new round of exams. It is stressful to consider taking on that work twice a year into perpetuity.

To get a broader measure of the school's progress, Jose and his staff do more than rely on the state report card that shows testing results. They also examine what their students are saying, the overall instruction, student behavior, and public comments.

First and foremost, for years we have relied on the state report card. Second, we survey our students each year about the effectiveness of our behavioral support system and their interpersonal connectedness to staff and to each other.

The state report card results this year were terrible. The worst we have ever had. This is despite the fact that in my observation, there were no significant declines in our instruction or behavior, and that by every other standard we appeared to be improving (we are growing in enrollment, we get good reviews from the general public, student attendance remains very strong, incidents of violence remain low). This change seems directly and entirely attributable to the implementation of a new test to evaluate what the old test evaluated.

Our student survey shows that students generally know what is expected of them at school, they feel they are treated fairly, and they have at least one adult staff member whom they can go to in a time of need or concern. These are important metrics for us, and we use them to make tweaks in our school culture each year. This focus on who our students are, and how they feel about the work we are doing, remains important to us, even as it gets lost in state and federal assessments of our work.

To repeat, these two highly successful leaders, Principals Jose and Dostal, make a common point: They measure their progress by more than their test scores. Even in this age of extreme testing accountability, they still try to gauge their overall progress in how well they are developing young people. That is the most important core value of educators. As school leaders move through disruptions, they need to constantly remind staff that their over-arching goal is the safety, development, and happiness of students. This has been one of the great motivators since the first days of teaching, and it's still very much a force today, when things are changing more rapidly than ever before.

This brings us to one of the most important questions of this era: *What are the constant reforms, testing, labeling, and micromanaging of the curriculum and teaching methods doing to our teachers?*

A TEACHER'S VIEW: THE FREEDOM TO TEACH

Krista Taylor is an award-winning teacher in Jose's school, and she, too, has seen the changes in schools, including changes in what she is expected to do in her own classroom. She eloquently sums up the challenges encountered by classroom teachers who have seen their curriculum and instruction evolve from deep, original units to standards-based instruction designed to prepare students for state assessments.

Stories From Exceptional Educational Leaders

Krista Taylor, Teacher
Gamble High School
Cincinnati, Ohio

When I began teaching outside of Boston in 1995, the State of Massachusetts was just starting to create something called "state standards." A lot of my instruction was focused around the development of what was called in those days "critical thinking skills." I built a whole unit (for high school students) around studying the concept of family as it was presented in children's picture books. For the culminating project, the whole class worked together to write, illustrate, and publish a picture book depicting every kind of family structure we could imagine. We then gave our book to a first-grade class as a gift. It was a great unit.

(Continued)

My students explored all kinds of things in the process, worked on many language arts concepts, gained validation for their own family structures, and created a final product that they were proud of. But I'd never do that today. It takes too much time and would fulfill few of the requirements of the Common Core State Standards.

These days, the weight of high-stakes testing seems to inform every decision. There is little done in a classroom simply for the sheer joy of doing it. In many ways it feels as if we are all marching in lockstep toward an externally determined goal. I am grateful to teach in a school where I feel somewhat protected from all of that—where we have been able to take the state and district requirements and meet them in a way that matches the goals we have for ourselves at a building level.

So much change is thrown at teachers each year without sufficient preparation or training that it is impossible to keep up. No one can properly integrate multiple sets of new content, materials, or instructional strategies when provided with only an hour or two of training and an expectation that, from initiation, these new models will be implemented with proficiency and fidelity. It seems that just as soon as we get our feet under us regarding new changes, they are pulled away and changed again. Over time, this leads to a deep cynicism and a disengagement from all reform efforts as a means of self-protection.

There are some positive impacts. Looking at data can be beneficial if it is examined in a well-rounded manner that includes many means of measurement. Additionally, reform efforts have led me to increase rigor in my personal practice and to seek methods to support struggling learners in rising to this elevated level of instruction.

There is a pervasive feeling of helplessness in the face of school reform efforts. Teachers are losing control over the profession they hold so dear. We feel as if we have to fight tooth and nail to maintain a focus on development of the whole-child. While no one, including those in the school reform movement, openly states that they are against this practice, it is simply not possible to do all the things that are expected of us, and the high-stakes nature of testing winds up being the biggest driver of all school decisions.

Additionally, time (or the lack thereof) is very concerning. As noted above, looking at data is a beneficial practice that has emerged from the reform movement, but properly collecting, analyzing, and presenting that takes a tremendous amount of time. Educators have been given no extra time or extra staff to assist with this. We are only adding more to a workload that was already more than full.

Certainly, a simplified look at data through bubble test results is much more expedient, and this is what we are being pushed to rely on, but this is an inadequate and unreliable indicator of academic growth. There are broader ways of examining data, but we can't keep asking teachers to do more in the same amount of time. Teacher shortage appears to be an increasing concern, which is trending to become a critical issue in a few more years. Low morale tied to overwork and a lack of personal control are huge challenges that must be overcome in order to attract young people to this noble profession.

Protect your teachers from a singular focus on testing outcomes.

- *Remind them every chance you get that they are making a difference in the life of a child.*

- *Acknowledge them for the value of this work—even, or perhaps especially, on the days when it feels like everything is futile.*

- *Children may not respond to guidance in an hour, or a day, or a week, or even a year, but everything teachers give to them influences them somehow, and teachers may never know the true impact they have— so tell them. They need it now more than ever.*

Here's the lesson for all administrators in a time of constant education reforms: Great teachers like Taylor should be free to teach; great administrators should help their staff balance test data with all the other remarkable things they do for kids. If schools are going to survive the transition into hyper-change, then they will still need experienced, caring teachers at the forefront of managing change. The only way teachers can survive is if their desire to teach is nurtured by leaders and protected from being killed off through standardization.

TEACHER PREPARATION: DRILLING DOWN INTO THE DATA

Dr. Jennifer Regelski is an assistant professor, secondary and STEM education, at the Educators College at Marian University in Indianapolis, Indiana. Earlier in her career she was a high school science teacher, but now she prepares university students. She has seen some parts of teacher preparation remain the same, while other parts have changed dramatically to deal with test-centered reforms. First, she recounts her own student teaching experience, one to which many teachers trained in the 20th century can relate.

Stories From Exceptional Educational Leaders

Dr. Jennifer Regelski, Assistant Professor of Secondary and STEM Education

Educators College, Marian University

Indianapolis, Indiana

In the late '90s, I attended a small liberal arts college in the Midwest to obtain my post-baccalaureate teaching credentials after graduating a few years prior with a bachelor's degree in zoology. During my teacher education program, I took the required basics: classroom management, assessment, educational psychology, educational technology, one course on diversity, and a general methods course before my final semester. During my "senior year" courses in general methods and classroom management, there were built-in field components in which I completed some observations in both a middle and high school. Those were simply observations with a few instances of going over homework or helping to play a review game. Essentially, my entire teacher prep program was all in preparation for my culminating project: student teaching. Student teaching was considered to be a survival of the fittest. My cooperating teacher had a sink-or-swim mentality and after he observed me teach on my own a couple of times, he went on sabbatical, in a figurative sense. After I taught a lesson first period, he and I sat down to troubleshoot what to do differently in our second period study hall so that I could make the necessary changes before third period. Luckily, I swam and swam well, or at least well enough.

The contact I had with the university during my student teaching was limited. A few times, I met with my supervisor, a science education faculty member at the university. She observed me teach four or five times over the semester, after which she provided feedback on what I was doing well and what I could improve upon. Unlike today, there was no rubric and just a few paragraphs of narrative offering suggestions for improvement and examples of what I was doing well. I also attended a seminar course to discuss the portfolio we needed to fill with evidence of our teaching. We submitted this at the end of the semester and someone gave us the rubber stamp that we needed to pass the internship. I went on to successfully teach high school science for 14 years.

Dr. Regelski says the overall format of the teacher prep programs—compartmentalized courses that lead to field experiences, internships, and student teaching—is similar to what she experienced two decades ago. She thinks a huge improvement could be to add more supervision for preservice teachers in practicum or field exercises and to more thoroughly vet the cooperating teachers to ensure the university students are getting the very best in mentorship. But she also sees how the programs today have adjusted with the national reform initiatives.

Teacher prep programs are dutifully following state and national standards put forth by the state boards of education and by accrediting bodies, respectively. The age of accountability has not left higher education untouched. These programs are also consistently revising their curriculum to teach current methods, research-based practices, and high-impact teaching strategies. Modern pedagogy is becoming more aligned with current research on learning, such as brain-based strategies. Since the implementation of No Child Left Behind and requirements for Adequate Yearly Progress, there has been much more emphasis on assessment and data-driven decision making, and this is reflected in not only assessment courses but in accreditation standards as well. . . . Things have changed but I personally believe more change is needed.

Another professor who has seen the disruptions in teacher preparation is Dr. Rae White, the chair of the Education Department at Muskingum University in New Concord, Ohio. She, too, has seen the impact of accountability and its reach into the university programs.

Stories From Exceptional Educational Leaders

Dr. Rae White, Chair of the Education Department

Muskingum University

New Concord, Ohio

As I began teaching in the 1970s the focus was on assisting each student and centered on reading skills (fluency, decoding, and comprehension), and the content was very much determined at the school building or district level. This preceded national and state-level standards, and contrary to statements that it was disorganized, teachers actually did look to see what pieces of literature were age and grade-level appropriate and they tailored instruction to help each student understand complex texts. As with any initiative there are pros and cons, so in the advent of standards, specific expectations were articulated that helped coordinate the curriculum, and as students transferred from one district to another, there was a parallel curriculum across Ohio. Along with the standards came a hyperfocus on ensuring that everyone was following them with fidelity and ensuring all students retained the new content as they moved through the advancing grades—thus standardized testing accompanied the movement. The impact on teacher preparation was clear as colleges and universities connected with the kindergarten through Grade 12 school buildings for field experiences and student teaching.

The most significant difference in the past 30 years is the push for oversight, reporting, and accountability on everyone's part. Currently education preparation providers (EPPs) have to report to a national accrediting body titled CAEP—the Council for Accreditation of Educator Preparation. . . . Currently each college or university that has a teacher preparation program in America is addressing the new CAEP standards, developed in 2013, and is to submit a self-study report and schedule a site visit to present required data to a team of examiners who verify the results and recommend, or not, that accreditation be granted. The intensity and formality of the entire process is arduous, but it does ensure that only quality programs will continue to prepare teachers in each state.

The teacher preparation in the preservice programs in American universities has never been so focused, efficient, and effective; yet many of their concerns now have to do with their accountability systems and preparing college students to enter a system of high accountability based on standardized testing.

What if teachers could effectively use a strong standards-based curriculum that allowed creative, individualized methods of assessing student success in the standards? Think of how it could change preservice programs, teaching, and student lives.

It's time to start looking at new options for kids.

PIVOTING TO A FUTURE OF RAPID CHANGE

Look at what these educators who serve at different levels are telling us: They are living in an education system that is becoming increasingly regimented in tests, labels, and accountability. At the same time, we know today's businesses realize the secret to survival is creativity and the ability to quickly pivot to new ways of operating.

In this era that requires extreme flexibility, we are locking our educators more tightly than ever into a 20th century accountability model of mass assessments. The world is heading in one direction, and American education is headed in the opposite direction. As the world is becoming more individualized, our schools are becoming more regimented. While the world increasingly values entrepreneurial thinking, our education system values test scores.

And here's a point lost on so many politicians and education leaders: If we could somehow help every student in America achieve the highest scores on his or her tests, that would not guarantee success in a 21st century global community. Yes, it would help for students to have a stronger foundation in the core tested areas, but testing and labels will not help a student be creative, use technology in new ways, and have a mindset that can shift thinking from the year 2040 to 2050 and beyond.

How will this end? Will the leaders and politicians who have created the current system one day realize they need a new model that combines high standards and flexibility? Or will they just continue to assert that the answer to hyper-change is more mass testing? If the current system of high-stakes standardized assessment and labeling is continued, will it come rattling down in the next decade, or will it just quietly implode as students and their families finally say "Enough!" and seek out education options that might not exist today?

Now more than ever, our education leaders and policymakers who have the power to steer education must value flexible mindsets. They must understand what is happening to the world through disruptions and form a road map to the future built around creativity and adaptability. Some of the alternatives to tests have been discussed in the education field: individual capstone projects instead of graduation tests; digital portfolios that track a student's growth instead of tracking it through adequate yearly progress in testing; adapting a system to fit the needs of the individual student instead of giving a standardized test like the one given to thousands of others. Or just don't give so many tests. Technology and artificial intelligence will open new possibilities and create assessment options in the future that can be more effective and user-friendly—if they are developed and used.

Today, our school leaders and teachers must keep alive the flame of hope that drove them into education. And they must understand what is happening and be ready to rapidly pivot when new reform doors are opened.

Tips for Leading Schools in an Age of Constant Education Reforms

⚡ In this era of high-stakes testing, take care of your students. Make your school a safe place where their emotional and physical needs are met.

⚡ Keep your students at the center of instruction. Their 21st century academic needs, not the needs of the educators, should drive instruction.

⚡ Know where your students are going after they graduate from your school system. Make sure they have the skills they need to be successful.

- ⚡ Balance your culture's definition of success: The test scores are important, but so are all the other things you do in school, including the teaching of 21st century skills.

- ⚡ In the words of Krista Taylor: "Protect your teachers from a singular focus on testing outcomes. Remind them every chance you get that they are making a difference in the life of a child. Acknowledge them for the value of this work—even, or perhaps especially, on the days when it feels like everything is futile."

Chapter 5 Scenarios for Applying the CAT Strategy

Scenario 1: A new test has been implemented by the state. The new test is more difficult than the last test, and there are questions in the education community about its content and reliability. When the scores are sent to the school several months after the test has been given, they are lower in almost every category at every grade. The school's accountability rating will be lowered. This is particularly hard for the school because in the previous year the school had been recognized by the state for its high test scores. Many other schools around the state are also seeing an overall drop in test scores.

Cope: In the days after the test scores are released, the principal reassures students, parents, and teachers that the teaching in the school has been done at a high level and students are still being prepared for a successful future. The principal stresses that the test is a new one and the school will study the data, adjust curriculum and teaching strategies, and work to improve scores in the future. The principal continues to stress the need to focus on the required testing, as well as promoting global skills and helping them have an entrepreneurial mindset. The principal reminds all parties that the mission of educating the whole child is still in place.

(Continued)

(Continued)

Adjust: In the weeks after the release of test scores and lower accountability ratings, the principal works with teachers to more clearly define where improvements in test preparation need to be made. The principal also continues to remind the teachers to be true to their core values that go beyond testing and ratings. Instead of having the test preparation consume the staff and to prepare for future change, the principal announces the need to push more deeply into student use of technology and global readiness.

Transform: In the following months, the principal continues to lead the test preparation and global readiness efforts, and the principal constantly reminds the staff to nurture the whole child. The principal uses the year as an opportunity to help teachers understand the world is changing, testing and accountability are fluid initiatives, and they should be prepared for more changes in the future.

Scenario 2: The state legislators are concerned about Internet safety for young people, so they pass a law that requires each school to implement 10 lessons per year on Internet safety. Teachers are concerned about losing instructional time, especially when each curriculum is so crowded and testing results are so important for teacher and school accountability ratings.

Cope: In the days after the law is passed, the principal has a staff meeting to discuss the parameters of the law and its intent. The principal asks for input from the staff for creative ways to comply with the law and to help students. The principal reminds teachers the law is meant to keep young people safe, and they should all work together to remind students about the dangers that can be found on the Internet. The principal then meets with student leaders to seek their input.

Adjust: In the following weeks, the principal consults with the teacher leadership team about the suggestions from the staff, and they devise a plan for creating the lessons and implementation.

The principal communicates with the president of the parent/teacher organization to get that person's input. The principal also shares the plan with student leaders for their input. The plan is finalized with the teacher leadership team and released to the students, staff, and community.

Transform: In the following months, the principal works with the leadership team to analyze the success of the lessons and where the school's digital citizenship plan could be improved for the following year. The principal checks discipline data, collects surveys of students, and checks anecdotal evidence about digital successes and transgressions. The principal talks with student leaders to get their feedback and suggestions. Before the school year ends, the principal and school leadership team have an improved version of the plan ready to be implemented in the following year.

ACTIVITIES TO TRANSFORM IN EDUCATION REFORM DISRUPTIONS

1. Principal Dostal reminds us of the words of David Bowie: "And these children that you spit on as they try to change their worlds are immune to your consultations. They're quite aware of what they're going through."

   What are the benefits and challenges for your students as they have gone through the NCLB, the Common Core, or ESSA and other reform efforts? How are they "immune" to it?

2. Do you feel your school has the right balance of being reform/test centered and student centered? Why or why not?

3. What is the feeling of the teaching staff toward the constant reform efforts? Is there, as Ms. Taylor says, a "pervasive feeling of helplessness" in dealing with them? What can you do to help your teachers? What suggestions do they have?

(Continued)

(Continued)

4. How can you provide more differentiation or personalized learning to help students move beyond the limiting goals of standardized testing?

Learn From the Past

Study your actions from the past. Use the following chart to reflect on education reform disruptions and what you did to cope, adjust, and transform with them. Read the prompts on the left and fill in the boxes on the right. Feel free to work through this process with multiple disruptive events to look for patterns and clues for future success.

PROMPTS FOR UNDERSTANDING	YOUR DISRUPTIVE EVENT
List the education reform event that had a major impact on your school and culture. For example, it might be the release of test scores or accountability ratings for the Common Core, Race to the Top, ESSA, or a state or local initiative. Or perhaps it's the implementation of a new set of curriculum standards.	
How did you help your staff cope in the days immediately following the event?	
How did you adjust your practices or policies in the weeks after the event?	
How did you transform your philosophy or your staff's philosophy to better deal with future education reforms?	
Looking back, what went well?	
What could have gone better?	
Is there anything else you or your staff learned by going through the event?	
Do you think you and your staff are better prepared to deal with future education reform initiatives? Why or why not?	

Generational Differences

Leading Boomers, X, Y, and Z in New Learning Spaces

Once schools are in the hands of teachers who were born in Gen Z, only then do I think we'll truly start to see the notion of formal education evolve.

—Meegan Bennett, Learning Environment Consultant

Before the waves of disruptions, we didn't think about differences in generations. We just had two generations: the older generation in the teaching staff and the younger generation in the students. Then things started to accelerate, the world became disrupted, and generations in America began to exhibit different characteristics. In some ways, the generations have grown up in different versions of America, and it has shaped their view of the world. We have reached a point in our schools where members of the eldest generation, the baby boomers (who are the kids of the Greatest Generation, the group that survived the Great Depression, defeated fascism, and won World War II), are in senior leadership positions presiding over schools where the enrollment is made up of Gen Z kids who'd rather watch a YouTube video than read a history book.

Today's American teenagers spend up to 9 hours per day online playing games, watching videos, texting, and connecting through social media. Younger kids spend up to 6 hours per day online; some 13-year-olds check social media 100 times per day (Hadad). The baby boomers can try to talk with the kids about their generational differences—if they can get the kids off of Snapchat long enough to chat in person.

And the generational differences are not just between the oldest and youngest groups in our schools. As administrators try to connect with Gen Z, they have to think about the philosophical views of three different generational layers within the teaching staff: the baby boomers, Gen X, and Gen Y (also known as millennials).

Our schools are adjusting to this natural shift: New generations bring new views and needs. There is turbulence in change, and to adjust successfully to generational disruptions, we need to know more about the groups—and understand how they should work together to create new methods and types of learning space designed for our youngest generation, today's students.

A CLOSER LOOK AT FOUR GENERATIONS IN OUR SCHOOLS

To lead multiple generations of teachers, administrators need to understand that each generation is a different layer. These layers stack on each other, from the baby boomers to Gen Z.

Our teachers on the verge of retirement are the baby boomers; they were born between 1945 and 1964. They were the first generation to grow up with television, credit cards, divorce, and the fear of nuclear weapons. They were the hippies, the generation that wanted to change the whole world (Novak). Teachers of this generation are the ones who have seen the waves of disruptions in society, and they have taught through the waves of American school change. They remember the era when standardized tests were infrequently given and there were no accountability ratings. They often talk about the "good old days" before their curriculum was scripted and their job security was tied to test scores. They might use technology, but they tend to say they just don't understand it. And here's a key point for administrators: While some baby boomers have embraced change, a significant number see the current disruptions and say, "It's hard enough today. I don't want to be a part of the schools that are coming. I'm glad I'll be retired before all of that happens!" In other words, a significant chunk of our most experienced generation of educators is stepping to the sidelines and not leading or embracing change. This would create a difficult hurdle for any workforce in any field. Administrators must lead with the baby boomers who are on board and fill the void left by the leadership absence of others.

Then came Generation X from 1965 to 1980. They are the latch-key kids who grew up with a certain cynicism about the government and the rest of the world. They tend to be individualistic and more concerned with what's going on around them than with saving the world (Novak). They are less likely to defer to a principal or to someone else's view. The early Gen Xers in teaching entered the workforce during the Accountability Age; they've known standardized testing since their first days in the classroom.

Generation Y, also known as the millennials, arrived from 1981 to 2000. They are the children of 9/11 and helicopter parents, the ones who want to work in teams in a casual environment. These are the teachers who have grown up with technology and can do the best job of conversing with today's students about apps. Nick Friedman, a blogger for Pearson Labs, has written:

> *As digital natives, Millennial teachers are used to engaging with a wide variety of content forms on multiple platforms. The desktop computer in the corner of the classroom? That's old school. Millennials flourish with new hardware and new apps.*

> *Victoria Olson, who teaches at West Langley Elementary School in British Columbia, Canada, integrates technology "into everything I teach." The 27-year-old has the students in her third- and fourth-grade classrooms create digital portfolios on iPads and Chromebooks. "Developing content on creation-based applications provides deeper learning," says Olson. Among the software they use are Google Apps for Education, Kidblog, and PicCollage. However, she warns, "Ed tech shouldn't just be about the app, it should be what students do with the apps."*

But leading millennials can be a challenge for administrators. Principal Kristin Barker recently wrote an article for ASCD in which she detailed the travails and joys of working with millennial teachers.

I wish I knew then what I know now: these Millennial educators have different needs and expectations. As a card-carrying member of Generation X, I grew up learning how to be self-reliant, independent, and resourceful. However, like many other Gen-Xers, I became a hypervigilant parent who provided support to my kids that I wasn't provided with when I was a child. I created schedules, activities, and play dates, and I managed almost every aspect of their lives. In essence, I raised the teachers that I am now hiring.

Millennials are sometimes called Generation Y, which is fitting because that is a question they often ask—why? As a new principal, I was completely unprepared for their frequent questions and sometimes constant need for approval. At the same time, I was delighted by their optimism, collaboration, and ability to move effortlessly in the world of digital literacy. There was so much to love about my new teachers, yet they all chose to leave. To quote them—why? What could I have done differently? (Barker)

Barker cites researcher Denise Teague in the *Delta Kappa Gamma Bulletin* in saying school leaders can take three steps to help millennial teachers successfully transition into a school staff:

1. Expand induction activities. Most traditional onboarding practices are not explicit enough or embedded deeply enough to help millennial teachers understand the needs of professional teaching.

2. Create more collaboration opportunities between senior and younger teachers. Millennial teachers might not appreciate what the senior teachers can offer, and millennials tend to bond tightly together.

3. Add value for them. Millennial teachers want to be heard and offer their expertise in schools. Mixing them into training and helping break down walls with senior staff will help them feel valued.

And today, we have Gen Z students, the Starbucks Generation, the ones who have grown up with the Internet and constant connectivity. They leave their traditional toys at an earlier age—because they start switching to digital devices (Novak). They have cell phones, they have video game consoles, they connect online with people around the world, and they have a plethora of entertainment options at their fingertips. They have short attention spans, and teachers must work harder than ever to adjust their teaching to keep these students engaged. For Gen Z, technology in the classroom is not an option; it's a necessity. They often have things their way, on their time, and where they want them. School is too often an unnatural place where they turn off their devices, power down, conform, and sit in straight rows.

Let's look at these generational challenges, and especially the need to reinvent learning space, through the eyes of four experts in different positions: a school administrator, a learning environment consultant, an architect, and a furniture/design CEO who is reimagining his role as he helps school leaders design Gen Z learning spaces.

THE ADMINISTRATOR LEADING GEN Z AND GENERATIONS OF TEACHERS

A leader who has experienced the challenge of leading multiple generations within the teaching staff is Kate Thoma, an administrator at New Albany Elementary School in New Albany, Ohio.

Stories From Exceptional Educational Leaders

Kate Thoma, Administrator
New Albany Elementary School
New Albany, Ohio

There is a huge difference in the approach of teachers based on their generation. While there are always outliers, I struggle to get our older generation of teachers to see the value in technology and how it can enhance student learning. That sounds like I'm stereotyping, and like I said, it isn't true of the entire group. I just feel so much resistance to trying different things because "they won't work." Whether it's a schedule change, a

(Continued)

(Continued)

classroom design change, using Google Apps for Education, using Twitter for Professional Learning, the list goes on and on. I do, however, want to say that I think it's possible to break through to this age range. While it may not be the breakthrough I hope for, it is a small step. I think back to a course I was teaching this summer where the assignment was to explain what design thinking was in a way that could be shared with others. It could have been any shareable way . . . any way! To watch this group of educators problem solve how they were going to share their knowledge was quite the learning opportunity for me. Some all but had a breakdown over not being able to use PowerPoint (which they could have and then uploaded to Google Slides, but that was too much for them) or stressing about what exactly I wanted them to say about design thinking. In the end, all 25 participants had a shareable explanation of design thinking that included Google Slides, Infographics, Prezi, and other methods. But . . . there is definitely a difference in generations' willingness to examine our approach to teaching; the solution is to provide them a safe place to break down their own barrier.

She also understands the different approach needed to reach Gen Z. As a teacher, technology coach, and administrator, she's adjusted practices to meet student needs.

I think the biggest shift for me personally has been diving into the use of social media. I've had to plug into life differently so that I can understand and empathize with today's learners. As I shifted from a technology coach, back into the classroom, then to an administrator role, I've been lucky enough to try to apply various types of technology in the classroom and in my professional learning. Students today don't unplug, and now I understand why. Understanding the "why" allows me to plan differently within the classroom, therefore planning differently for staff. Within my summer workshop series, "The Foundations of Innovation," I've been able to connect our staff to new ideas, concepts, and networks of other professionals that are changing their status quo and how we do school. None of this, however, would have been possible without me taking the first leap. I live by the mindset that I will not ask others to do what I myself am not willing to do. That holds true for staff and students, and so I strive to make sure that along with the why, I am practicing on a daily basis what I hope my teachers will attempt to do, learning 24/7 by being connected.

Thoma also has studied her students and encourages teachers to redesign classrooms to keep up with changing learning styles.

I think it's critical that we redesign all schools and spaces to match where this generation learns best. School cannot continue to look as it has for the past 100 years. When you ask students where they like to work they'll tell you, honestly. If our spaces don't have similarities to where they like to learn, we are already encouraging our students to check out. We cannot change our teaching without changing our space. My favorite quote about space is from the book Make Space *by Scott Doorley and Scott Witthoft. (I highly recommend everyone have a copy of this book. It is full of ideas and inspiration.) In it they say, "Space is the body language of an organization," and that quote has lived with me since I first read it. I look around constantly and think about what our space is saying about us. What does my office say to students? Does it show what I value? Is it a place where students want to be? . . . What does your space say about you?*

Thoma raises a great point when it comes to space redesign: School leaders should do it to meet the needs of Gen Z and not just to design a new space because it's a trend. She based her designs on research and practical observations.

Another key to success is to involve key stakeholders in the process, especially students. It's a powerful message to say, "We spoke to our learners, and this is what they told us. . . ." Teachers need to have a voice, and parents and community members must be consulted. The worst thing a school leader can do with space redesign is to do it alone without input and then have students and teachers walk into the space and have no idea what has happened. Now more than ever, administrators must create partnerships that can provide input and assist with training and messaging.

THE LEARNING ENVIRONMENT CONSULTANT WITH AN OPTIMISTIC VIEW

Another educator who has studied Gen Z is Meegan Bennett, a former teacher who is now a learning environment consultant in Denver, Colorado. She understands the pedagogical demands of preparing a space that fits 21st century learners.

**Meegan Bennett (@meegsbennett),
Learning Environment Consultant**

Denver, Colorado

I think the most significant changes in learning spaces since I entered the profession in 2002 have been in school furniture. Of course there have been huge shifts in technology, but school furniture has been the "silent curriculum" game changer for many classrooms. There are so many more options in the types of materials, surfaces, sizes, shapes, and colors, mostly due to the technological advances in the way furniture is manufactured. And furniture manufacturers are also doing their homework. They're beginning to understand the importance of research in education and curriculum trends; there's significant product development with ergonomics, such as furniture that allows for more movement (both for the student to wiggle and the furniture to reconfigure), and it's forcing them all to go to market with products that are truly innovative and different. . . .

The impact of new furniture on Gen Z will depend on whom you ask. If you ask a Gen Zer, they're likely already comfortable with (and probably expect) some level of a coffee shop-like experience in their education. This generation knows that the coolest places to work are the ones that have the coolest spaces, with lots of variety and choice of where, when, and how to work. I don't think they are the slightest bit fazed by the notion of flexible and innovative furniture; they just intuitively know how to use it for their needs as learners.

Bennett is optimistic about the future of education; she sees the greatest change agents of all coming into schools in the near future: Gen Z when they enter the classrooms as teachers.

I think as a whole, districts are still wondering how to "keep up with all the changes" that are happening right now! So many districts I've worked with seem to say they're doing innovative things, but the pace of educational innovation can't even touch the pace of technology innovation, and I think that's the biggest struggle they all face. Once schools are in the hands of teachers who were born in Gen Z, only then do I think we'll truly start to see the notion of formal education evolve. The next generation of teachers will be the biggest agents of change and the new pace setters for educational innovation, because the generation of students they will serve will have unfathomable access to technology and tools by then. Their schools will look and feel entirely different because the "factory model" of education will be a long forgotten phase.

Educators often struggle as they move from a fixed mindset of straight rows to one of optimum flexibility. Bennett has four quick tips for administrators who are thinking of redesigning their learning spaces.

1. *Look around.*

   Walk around your school and look closely at how the furniture is being used (or not used) in classrooms, common spaces, the library, the cafeteria, and offices. Is it ergonomic, comfortable, and selected to match the learning activities happening in the space?

2. *Start early.*

   Lead times for furniture can be as long as 8 to 12 weeks. April through July is the busiest time of year for furniture manufacturers. Plan ahead to ensure furniture is delivered when you need it and then add a "buffer" week just in case.

3. *Get organized.*

   Keep track of all the items you're interested in or are planning to order. Start a spreadsheet. If you involve a furniture provider who has a designer on staff, this will all be done for you in the design phase of the project.

4. *Work with a furniture provider who cares.*

   Check with your district facilities or purchasing department as to which furniture dealers you can order from. It's also a good idea to know if the furniture provider will need to submit a bid or an RFQ (request for qualifications). You may have options when it comes to furniture providers, but remember, you can't put a price on customer service. Try to find a dealer who will ask the right questions, such as, "What's your vision for this space?" or "Tell me about the students, teachers, and community at your school," or "What types of activities happen here?"

THE EXPERIENCED ARCHITECT
WITH A VISION FOR CHANGE

Gary Sebach, AIA, is the director of Architectural Design at OHM Advisors in Columbus, Ohio. When he began his career, he was asked to design schools to meet the needs of the Industrial Age; however, within the past decade he's seen a shift among educators who are seeking help in designing spaces for the 21st century.

Stories From Exceptional Educational Leaders

**Gary Sebach, AIA Director
of Design, Architecture**

OHM Advisors

Columbus, Ohio

I designed my first school addition in 1986 and it was simply a long corridor with classrooms on each side. That was the solution that had preceded me and would continue as the norm for years to come. I went to high school in the late '70s and the building was very progressive, with 80% of the walls able to be folded away. The irony was that they were rarely folded away and the classrooms functioned as isolated rooms with silo-ed programs. It wasn't until the early 2000s that I fully realized the concept of the folding walls and why I think it failed to be used as it was envisioned. Today, we see a shift to more collaborative and flexible classroom configurations, but the big difference is now it is a student-centered environment and not a teacher-centered environment.

Sebach also has seen how the different generations deal with learning space, from the boomers to the students; it's the older members of the education community who have trouble shifting their paradigms.

Often, it's the legacy teachers that are hesitant and resistant to change, and if they choose to teach in the same way, even in a new school, then we've failed to fully realize the potential of 21st century education concepts. . . . Unfortunately, sometimes its district leaders and parents who don't support the concept of 21st century learning. Recently I had a well-intended board member talk to me about the importance of having dictionaries and a more traditional library in case a student needed to look up something. I argued that technology has replaced the need for dictionaries and that students don't have to go to the library to access information. It's hard sometimes to get teachers and district leaders to think about how we should and will be teaching in the future, and not be thinking about how we taught in the past or even in the present.

He also points out that we are heading toward a more informal society and that learning spaces in schools are mirroring the trend being seen in progressive companies as they design spaces for workers to foster creativity and encourage them to collaborate and communicate.

There are many authors that talk about the cultural shift from "owning things" to "experiencing things." Workplace and education are also shifting to be more about the experience of working and learning. . . . To me, a school will always be a place to help develop your skills, thinking process, and understanding of information. Humans need collaboration and connectivity to help develop cognitive skills. Just because we have easy access to information anytime, anyplace doesn't mean we know what to do with it or that we know if it's accurate. As schools develop in the future they will have to be more than an assembly of standard classrooms; they will have to support the notion of the "experience" of education.

Sebach finished with a great point for all 21st century educators: Schools must be places where students experience concepts and are not just told about them. It used to be that students would hear constant lectures, watch teachers write on the chalkboard, and answer questions in textbooks. Now they have to be up, moving around, swiping through screens, discussing the content, and creating something about it. Ultimately, Gen Z schools must be places where students can immerse themselves in education.

THE CEO ON A JOURNEY: A NEW GENERATION AND A NEW MISSION

Ira Sharfin is the CEO of Continental Office, a company in Columbus, Ohio, that specializes in helping its corporate customers, including schools, design spaces that fit their unique needs. He has seen many changes in the past decade as Gen Z students have disrupted the traditional learning space designs.

Stories From Exceptional Educational Leaders

Ira Sharfin, CEO

Continental Office

Columbus, Ohio

Today, K12 school districts are looking for opportunities to create unique spaces that provide a better learning environment for their students, in a way mirroring what higher education institutions are doing. I can tell you that we haven't sold a hard, plastic static chair in the past 2 or 3 years. Instead they are buying ergonomic chairs and desks that encourage movement. . . . Allowing the students to get up, move around is the best way many of our clients have found to keep their students' attention. This holds true with college students as well. . . .

The challenge for many K12 districts is finding the budget to invest in these new environments. They spend lots of money on creating new schools and then often end up having to value engineer their furnishings to meet overall budgets. This is the wrong approach. They should be asking themselves, "What types of spaces would create the best possible learning environment for our students now and over the next 5 years?" . . . The fact is, it's a much more strategic issue than 10 or 15 years ago when the goal was simply procuring low-cost furniture to fill up a new or remodeled school building. And the stakes are much higher for colleges and universities, many of which are challenged by attracting top-notch students to an institution that costs upwards of $50,000 or more.

We believe the best approach is to take an outside/in view. What problem is our client trying to solve? How do they envision using the space? What forces or changes might impact these objectives in the next few years? The answer may be new furniture or flooring, or it may be branding to help tie everything together. It's really similar for our school clients as it is for corporate companies. However, with schools there's more of an open environment, so flexibility is often something we discuss (i.e., how many different ways might they use any given learning space).

Sharfin has seen a merging of corporate and education spaces; they are becoming more similar. Schools used to be where students learned something, and businesses were where adults often did repetitive tasks and made money. Now school leaders and business executives are understanding the space is not just where tasks are done; it is also a place where the tasks are created.

It's an interesting dynamic when you talk about corporate and educational environments in the same conversation. When I entered the industry in 2005, there were clear delineations between corporate and education . . . from the actual design of space, to the types of furniture and flooring specified. Today there's been such a convergence because corporate executives realize that they desperately need highly functioning and inspiring learning spaces. Many companies have dedicated training centers, but they tend to look like classrooms from 20 years ago. In other words, not very inspiring.

Corporations had been out in front of schools in terms of designing more contemporary spaces, but the gap is definitely closing. . . . Schools have adopted some of the collaboration spaces that many corporations have shifted to, such as coffee bars, lounges, and small quiet zones. Much like the corporate world, we're seeing schools embrace ergonomics and flexibility. Technology is changing the physical space as we're seeing things like computer labs and libraries disappear. These are being replaced with collaborative areas and lounging spaces. There's a limit since classroom time still dominates most of the day. However, I believe that student-centric learning will push the need for more collaborative spaces over the next 5 years. You can definitely feel it moving that way.

Finally, Sharfin has these words for school leaders about learning space in the future: The disruptions aren't over; they will continue to occur.

(Continued)

(Continued)

I personally think it (learning space) will continue to evolve. It will be more focused on creating the best possible experience for students and faculty members. Just like students, teachers have a choice in where they work. Beyond compensation, the work environment (inspiring spaces) will influence many employment decisions.

As Sharfin says, a key factor for millennials in choosing jobs is the work environment, and it will be an important element for Gen Z and all the generations that follow. As the gap increases between schools that are adapting their learning spaces and those that aren't, young teachers will gravitate to those schools that have implemented flex spaces and creative environments in classrooms. Ultimately, space redesign is not an option; it's a necessity for all 21st century schools.

Tips for Leading in Generational and Learning Space Disruptions

- ⚡ Expand induction activities to help millennial teachers understand more about professional school environments.

- ⚡ Create more collaboration opportunities between senior and younger teachers.

- ⚡ Value all generations of teachers, but know that millennial teachers want to be heard and offer their expertise in schools.

- ⚡ Redesign your learning space to meet the needs of Gen Z.

- ⚡ Involve all stakeholders to make sure they understand what is happening and can take ownership.

- ⚡ Focus your designs on Gen Z learning styles and today's more relaxed society, not just a desire to be part of a trend to create a new space.

- ⚡ Look around. See how furniture and space are being used.

- ⚡ Work with a furniture provider who cares about your school.

Chapter 6 Scenarios for Applying the CAT Strategy

Scenario 1: A principal hears a school in a nearby district is redesigning its learning space. The principal wonders if her district should also begin to rethink how it is using learning space for Gen Z. The principal's first thought is to immediately buy some new furniture and start redesigning some classrooms. However, the principal decides it would be more prudent to involve others in the process.

> **Cope:** The principal begins to talk with key players, such as the superintendent, teacher leaders, students, parents, and community members. Some of the educators have heard of space redesign efforts, and they are curious. The students tell the principal they would be in favor of creating new types of classrooms and meeting rooms and using hallways and other spaces differently. The parents and community members are supportive as long as the concept is educationally sound and affordable.
>
> **Adjust:** In the following weeks the principal forms a leadership group to assist her. She asks, "How do we use the space now? What do we know about Gen Z? Which spaces do we redesign in our school?" The group begins to gather information. It also researches the topic online to see what other schools, universities, and businesses are doing with their spaces. The group solicits the help of a leading architect who volunteers his time to help the group imagine the possibilities. It is decided two classrooms, a part of a hallway, and a part of the media center will be given new colors, various types of student-chosen furniture, and technology upgrades, and will be used differently.
>
> **Transform:** In the months after the space redesign decision is made, the principal works with the media center specialist, teachers, and students to understand the possibilities of how to use the new space. The team, including the students, helps with the selection of colors, furniture, and overall design. The school begins to purchase the furniture and other materials, and the educators and students report back to the committee on what

(Continued)

(Continued)

is working and what needs to be improved. The group uses their input as it expands its effort in the following year.

Scenario 2: It's September, and a new principal is starting the school year. The previous principal had redesigned the learning space of several classrooms prior to his departure, but he assured the new principal that key stakeholders had been involved in the process. However, in the first week of school, the new principal gets complaints from some students, parents, and teachers about the new space. They are asking questions like, "Why did this happen? How do we use this space? Why weren't we included?" The new principal realizes he has to quickly help everyone understand the new space and its uses and possibilities.

Cope: The principal immediately works with the teachers in the classroom to help them understand the space. He provides them with resources such as books, blogs, and websites. The principal also has a conference with the PTO president to tell him about the education process. The principal visits students in the newly redesigned rooms to reassure them and help them imagine what they can do in the space. Most students are very supportive, but some of the others need more conversations because they have only known traditional classrooms and need to be reassured about the new space.

Adjust: In the weeks after the issue is discovered, the principal continues to work with key stakeholders and solicits their input for moving forward. The principal makes frequent visits to the classrooms to observe and offer assistance. The principal meets privately with the teachers who use the space, and the principal makes the topic a key part of the next staff meeting to reaffirm commitment to the concept and solicit feedback from all teachers.

Transform: In the following months, the principal continues to work with the stakeholders and the teacher leadership team to pave the way for moving forward with more space redesign. They form a collective vision. The principal surveys the students in the rooms and asks them to list what they like about the spaces and how they compare with traditional spaces. The principal makes note of the lessons learned, and he constantly communicates the vision within the school and externally. The principal also uses social media to begin spreading the information and vision. The principal and leadership group form an action plan with a timeline and benchmarks for more space redesign in the following year.

 ACTIVITIES TO LEAD MULTIPLE GENERATIONS, EDUCATE GEN Z, AND DESIGN NEW TYPES OF LEARNING SPACE

1. What can you do to expand your induction activities and give all generations a voice in school operations?

2. How can you involve your staff generations, especially millennial teachers (who now compose the largest part of the American workforce), in your professional development activities?

3. Does your staff fully understand how Gen Z learns and their need for technology, social media, choice, and relevance? What systems or activities are in place to assist your teachers as they transition to teaching Gen Z?

4. Have you begun the redesign in learning space that will help Gen Z and future generations be creative, communicate, and collaborate?

Learn From the Past

Study your actions from the past. Use the following chart to reflect on generational disruptions and what you did to cope, adjust, and transform with them. Read the prompts on the left and fill in the boxes on the right. Feel free to work through this process with multiple disruptive events to look for patterns and clues for future success.

(Continued)

(Continued)

List an example of a generational difference that had a major impact on your school and culture. It might be a philosophical difference about teaching formed along generational lines or a new approach to learning space.

How did you help all your staff generations cope with it?

How did you adjust your practices or policies?

How did you transform your philosophy or your multigenerational staff's philosophy to better deal with it?

Looking back, what went well?

What could have gone better?

Is there anything else you or your staff learned?

Do you think you and your staff are better prepared to deal with generational differences and space redesign? Why or why not?

Global Readiness

Preparing for the 2030s, 2040s, and Beyond . . .

We have to impress upon students that learning never stops, particularly for those wanting to find themselves self-sufficient as adults.

—Bill Daggett, Education Reformer

In the 1990s, Charles Rouse was the principal of Leander High School in Leander, Texas. It was a simpler time. While *A Nation at Risk* had ushered in the Accountability Age for American schools and standardized test scores were becoming the standard for measuring progress, teachers still taught a content- or concept-based curriculum. The curriculum was approved by the local school board, often because the units in the curriculum had always been taught in schools. For example, kids in elementary science classes built clay volcanoes that "erupted" when they mixed baking soda and vinegar, and high school freshmen all read Shakespeare's *Romeo and Juliet*, because it was believed that knowing about Romeo and Juliet was an important part of being educated. Of course, today we've moved from a concept-based curriculum to a skills-based curriculum. Teachers might still use clay volcanoes and teach Shakespeare, but it's done to help students understand a group of standards.

Rouse was one of the first principals in 1992 to actively embrace one of the first sets of standards to enter American schools, the

Secretary's Commission on Achieving Necessary Skills (SCANS) report. The study was an initial attempt by the U.S. Department of Labor to formally transition American school curricula to prepare graduates for entry into the emerging global economy. Remarkably, a quarter of a century later, the report's three priorities are still applicable for today's school leaders in an era of global disruptions.

1. *All American high school students must develop a new set of competencies and foundation skills if they are to enjoy a productive, full, and satisfying life.*

2. *The qualities of high performance that today characterize our most competitive companies must become the standard for the vast majority of our companies, large and small, local and global.*

3. *The nation's schools must be transformed into high-performance organizations in their own right.* (SCANS)

In addition, the SCANS report's five broad competencies are still pertinent: student use of resources, interpersonal skills, information usage, understanding systems, and technology application. It also stressed the need for basic skills in reading and math, higher level thinking skills, and interpersonal skills.

Even then, Rouse saw the need to transform our schools so our graduates could move from having a local view to having a robust global understanding. "If we don't change the way we do things," he said, "we're going to be out of business one day." As a principal, Rouse was known for his leadership ability and his vision; he was one of the first local global leaders. Today, the district has a high school named in his honor.

It used to be that the U.S. secretary of education was the chief proponent of all public schools in America. That, too, has changed. Twenty-five years after Rouse's prescient words, President Donald Trump tapped a school-choice advocate to be the secretary of education. Frustrated with the perceived lack of progress in public education, or simply looking at the failing public schools and sweeping all of public education aside with the same disruptive broom, the Trump administration placed the education of over 50 million students ("Fast Facts") in the hands of someone who has made a career of promoting charter schools at the expense of public school funding (Ganim and Tran).

The support of alternative education systems at high levels should be viewed as a serious threat by school leaders. If public schools are going to survive, their leaders must rapidly embrace two concepts to help their students be global ready in an age of disruption and global competencies.

1. They must expose their students to other cultures in the world.
2. They must give their students the skills to adapt in a lifetime in which learning never stops.

Schools used to focus on American history and government; now they must find a way to also teach about the rest of the world. They used to prepare students to live in the local community, in another part of the state, or perhaps in another part of America; now they must prepare students to live in another part of the globe in a future that's hard to imagine.

CONNECTING TO THE WORLD: GOING GLOBAL

It used to be that states had to be concerned only with how the graduates of their public schools were successful within the borders of the state. Those days are gone. Every state now recognizes the need to be plugged into the global economy and for its graduates to have the sophistication to compete and thrive in a global environment.

In 2013, the North Carolina Board of Education released a report in which it listed what had to be done to ensure its students were global ready. Some of the report's main points emphasize the following:

1. *We aren't preparing students for a global tomorrow; North Carolina is global today.*
2. *Pilot programs won't cut it. Preparing globally competent graduates requires a comprehensive approach.*
3. *To prepare our students for the world, we need to prepare their teachers. Making global education a priority means making teacher preparation and development a priority.*

4. *North Carolina was once a leader in language learning. It's time to return to the pole position.*

5. *Schools need peers and partners to move this agenda. Building networks of schools, districts, higher education, third-party providers, and the business and governmental communities is a critical step to ensuring strong practice and innovative ideas go beyond the schools and communities in which they originate. . . .*

6. *If it's not sustainable, it's not a strategy. Effective programs that are not affordable over the long run ultimately will not serve North Carolina students and society.* ("Preparing Students for the World")

All these points can be applied to individual schools. Principals and superintendents everywhere could take them and build a broad global readiness initiative around them.

Shifts School Leaders Need to Make to Ensure Students Are Global Ready

- Teachers need to know what it means to be global ready; global readiness needs to be a central pillar of professional development.

- In these times of tight budgets, offering international languages is critically important. These initiatives don't just promote language acquisition; they also offer windows into other cultures.

- A wide range of opportunities is available for students to virtually meet students in other states and other countries through filtered, online programs. Students are already competing against each other online in video games; now they can learn together.

- America is growing more diverse; it's easier to find guest speakers and new viewpoints in many communities.

- When feasible, students should travel abroad, or at least explore other countries and cultures virtually. At the high school level, some students have taken weeklong trips overseas in which they traveled through Europe or China. These trips, though costly and requiring caution, are more important than ever for young people to broaden their views of global societies.

- Virtual reality will continue to offer more options; students will soon be able to explore the Colosseum in Rome and the ancient streets of Beijing by looking into a device.

- Districts can ensure that a wide range of global literature is made available to students at various grade levels; reading offers students a chance to connect with other cultures in deep and profound ways.

- More events are being broadcast live around the world; students today have more opportunities than ever to stream them on their phones or through school networks (Larson).

Ultimately, schools can become global ready by shifting their emphasis from a singular focus on testing to a philosophy that balances testing, the teaching of global skills, and just as important, establishing a culture of global awareness. As the world flattens, it will be more imperative, and easier, to bring the world into America's classrooms. The challenge for educators is that the curriculum used to be static and predictable from year to year. Now teachers must be prepared to shift it daily or perhaps hourly as global opportunities arise.

A LOCAL GLOBAL PRINCIPAL WITH A GLOBAL VISION

A school leader with a firm grasp on establishing a global approach is Chris Lehmann, the founding principal of the Science Leadership Academy (SLA) in Philadelphia, Pennsylvania. He and his staff have established core values that guide their actions and are meant to help students become global citizens.

Chris Lehmann, Founding Principal

Science Leadership Academy (SLA)

Philadelphia, Pennsylvania

I think one of the keys . . . is to understand how the goal of active, engaged citizenship is the key to serving all these different masters. Our core values of inquiry, research, collaboration, presentation—and a powerful ethic of care—and reflection guide all our decisions at SLA. When those ideas are your North Star, you have to plan accordingly. And the thing about the tests is this—kids need critical reading skills to achieve that North Star. And they need to be able to use mathematical reasoning to attack many of the problems that we as a society face. So the tests become less of a distraction when we stop thinking of having to prep kids for the tests and instead think about the skills the tests purport to measure. Do I think the tests are an accurate description of student ability? No . . . not compared to the work we see them do every day in the school, but we give them their due and keep it moving.

Lehmann stresses the need to balance inquiry and care with testing. It's not about test scores in his school; it's about being able to thrive in a global culture. He wants his students to understand the world today and his teachers to understand the teaching and learning methods that prompt inquiry and curiosity.

The way to make sure kids understand that they are part of a global citizenry and a global economy is by creating the opportunities for students to engage in the world. And yes, that can mean trips to Cuba and Germany and the Dominican Republic and England—which are all trips we've done—but it can also mean social action campaigns in our hometown of Philadelphia. And it can mean creating PSAs about voting rights in Spanish for the Spanish-speaking community in Philadelphia. In all, the work we ask kids to do has to matter. We have to stop treating school as preparation for the real world and value the fact that the kids live in the real world already, and their ideas, their intellect, their passion can change the world today—not someday.

And the way to help teachers create those conditions is to create those conditions with and for teachers as well. Professional development can be action research. It must be embedded in the work of the day. And it cannot be sit-and-get. Professional development time should be vibrant and powerful and filled with debate and discussion about how to figure out the best way to make a school vision live in practice every day. And teachers can come together to build common language and common frameworks and common tools to help students be able to focus on the work, not on figuring out the game of school, where each teacher speaks their own language and has their own set of systems that make the day more bewildering to kids. When we create schools with the idea of inquiry into action, where adults and students alike feel that their work matters and the work, vision, and practices are shared, then we can create the conditions where students can unlock their own agency and become the fully realized citizens of our nation and our world that we so desperately need them to be.

THE GLOBAL SKILLS: MORPHING AND GROWING WITH THE TIMES

When America first began to recognize the impact of the global economy, an emphasis was initially placed on the teaching of global skills, especially critical thinking, creativity (which is sometimes paired with entrepreneurship), collaboration, and communication. Educators often refer to these "4Cs," but that's just the beginning. More skills are being added in different areas as the world becomes more complex; we should think of the 4Cs as Skills 1.0.

We are well into the second or third iteration of global skill listing. According to a recent article by Will Richardson in *Educational Leadership*, school leaders must take three critical steps to move forward in multiple areas.

- Schools should articulate the abilities needed by students so educators can have a clearer focus on 21st century teaching and learning. Examples of skills include gathering, organizing, and analyzing data; thinking analytically; applying a variety of strategies to solve problems; participating fully in society; and self-evaluation.

- Schools should create deep learning cultures to develop people who want to learn for the rest of their lives. Everyone in the school must be a learner, not just the students.

- Schools should allow students to pursue their own interests. We are in a world in which fields, including education, are being democratized; students should be empowered to help shape their own education.

Richardson points out the difficulty of adding a new set of practices in place of the "centuries of history, practice, and nostalgia that are such a deep part of the current narrative of schooling." Nostalgia should be found in movies and culture, not in our schools.

Even the foundation of our school curricula has shifted in this age of disruption. It used to be that the "3Rs" of reading, writing, and arithmetic formed the basis of all curricula. While those areas are still heavily tested, futurist Marc Prensky writes:

> *Like it or not, technology has become foundational to both education and life. Educators should think of technology in the same way they've long viewed reading—as a key to thinking about and knowing about the world. In fact, in the 21st century, technology is the key to thinking about and knowing about the world. Reading continues to be important— no one argues against teaching or learning it—but today, reading is no longer the number one skill students need to take from school to succeed.*
>
> *Technology is.*

TODAY'S CURRICULUM: SHIFTING TO GLOBAL SKILLS

Consider what's happened to the curriculum and teaching in American schools since *A Nation at Risk* was released and the world entered the Disruption Age. When American schools were in a concept-based curriculum, a typical unit in many grades and subjects would consist of

- an introduction by the teacher,
- a chapter to be read by the students,
- study questions at the end of the chapter over the content,
- a quiz,
- a review, and
- a summative test.

Now consider the list of 21st century skills listed by the Digital Citizenship Foundation and Apex Learning as being essential for students to be successful in life after graduation:

- Critical thinking
- Communication
- Growth mindset
- Self-directed
- Social and emotional skills
- Self-awareness
- Relationship skills
- Responsible decision making
- Social awareness and perspective taking
- Self-management
- Problem solving
- Reflective
- Flexible and adaptable
- Active learner
- Nimble
- Resourceful
- Project and task management
- Articulate strengths and areas of need
- Life management
- Curious and inquisitive
- Digital citizens
- Innovative and entrepreneurial
- Passionate and positive
- Embrace failure
- Analytical and evaluative
- Grit and perseverance
- Logic and reasoning
- Cross-cultural communication (Crockett)

Students no longer are supposed to sit still every day to read a textbook and then take a test to measure their knowledge. These skills need interaction, innovative teaching, multiple activities in each lesson, new ways of assessing, a different way of approaching the curriculum, and time for teachers to work together to share ideas.

And how do we know we are teaching all these skills? We must be methodical and dedicated to change. In many schools, the state standards are taught to prepare students for tests, and while some of the standards cross over into global skills, the emphasis is on covering the standards; the teaching of global skills is often an addition or an afterthought. In the most tightly written curricula, teachers can say exactly when and how they taught a standard. We must move to a system where they can do the same for the global skills. For example, how many times is collaboration taught? Or communication? How is creativity stressed, and how often? Are students really thinking critically? Are they truly making judgments and evaluating or creating systems, or are they just thinking at high levels within an advanced curriculum that is not applicable to real-world situations? How are they using technology? Is it redefining the assignment or just a new way of doing the old one?

We are moving into an era of hyper-change, and much of what our students see now will change dramatically, over and over, in their lifetimes. Global skills that allow students to process information and create new paths are no longer an option. Schools should identify the skills to be taught, and they must have a master plan for their implementation and assessment.

Our current standards are tightly in place because they lead to state assessments and accountability ratings; the global skills must be put into place because it's the right thing to do for students.

And we must move toward a system that evaluates global skills. A mantra of education that still holds true from the 20th century is: *What gets inspected gets respected.*

LIFELONG LEARNING IS NO LONGER OPTIONAL

Bill Daggett, EdD, has spent much of his career trying to help educators get their students global ready. He is the chairman and founder of the International Center for Leadership in Education. For the past 25 years, he and his staff have been hosting the Model Schools Conference, one of the premier gatherings for educators to discuss the latest trends in school improvement, particularly with regard to increasing rigor and relevance in student learning. In 2017, he released a white paper discussing one of the most important global skills our graduates will need to navigate the 21st century: the desire to keep learning.

Are we challenging students to take the most rigorous and relevant courses that will best prepare them for their futures? Are we pushing them to choose college majors that are more likely to land them high-skilled jobs and help justify the expense (and debt) of college? Or are we watching as they choose the more "comfortable courses" they feel will leave more time for enjoying their school experience without challenging their thinking?

Most students only sit before us for about nine months. I realize as individuals, we can only do so much in nine months. But if we all band together around shared goals for students beyond graduation, collectively we can have a dramatic and lifelong impact on our students' futures.

One of those goals must be to cultivate in all of our students an interest in and respect for lifelong learning. We have to impress upon students that learning never stops, particularly for those wanting to find themselves self-sufficient as adults. We will only be able to convince them of this if we can communicate why.

The reason this is so critical is because careers today are no longer the static, well-defined, linear things they once were. That small computer you toss into your purse every day or carry around in your back pocket has changed everything.

For about a year, I've been using the likes of Facebook, Alibaba, Airbnb, and Uber to illustrate this point in talks and speeches. Facebook is the world's largest media provider, but it owns no content. Alibaba is the world's largest seller of products, but it owns no inventory. Airbnb facilitates housing for more travelers than any other hotel company in the world, but it owns no properties. Uber is the world's largest provider of automobile transportation, yet it owns no cars. Each transition away from how these industries have historically operated represents a change in jobs and skills. (Daggett)

And these changes, as Daggett points out, will cause our world and that of our students to keep evolving. Let's not just think of the world of 2017; we have to get students ready for the global landscape they'll encounter in 2037, 2047, and 2057.

A MODEL FOR TRANSFORMING

Many states have created career centers (also known by their former term, *vocational high schools*) to prepare students for a changing world. These schools have always done what today's comprehensive high schools are attempting to do: focus heavily on practical skills needed to be successful in the work world and in life.

Traditional schools can learn some lessons from them.

The career-themed schools have shifted with the times. While some of their subjects that were popular 40 years ago, such as lawn mower repair and house painting, have been deleted, others have faced radical technology upgrades. For example, auto repair and drafting are now computer aided and require a strong computer literacy component, reflecting the high-tech shift in the world of work. Today, entry into the schools requires more than just mechanical aptitude; a competency in core subjects is often a necessity, along with a strong desire to collaborate and think creatively to solve problems.

If these schools can quietly and successfully shift their operations, can't the rest of America's K–12 schools?

William L. Wittman is the superintendent/CEO of the Tri-County Career Center in Nelsonville, Ohio. He has witnessed the changes taking place in education—especially those affecting career-based education. It used to be that students could get decent jobs without receiving advanced training in their high school years. But those days are gone, and career centers have moved aggressively to keep up with the times.

William L. Wittman, Superintendent/CEO
Tri-County Career Center
Nelsonville, Ohio

No longer can one just graduate from high school with basic skills and gain living-wage employment. Advanced training needs to occur to provide opportunities. . . . Skill sets required in the global economy change constantly based on the employment needs of any given region of the state or country. Understanding the need to learn and use consumer skills is paramount to career programs. Employers will employ students who have an understanding in mathematics, reading, writing, computing, and personal communications. These skills provide additional capacity to any business or industry, providing a practical and common-sense awareness. In today's world, proper etiquette and interaction with others is vital to achieving a positive client base and work environment. At the career center, we train students as if they are on the job site. Attendance, attitude, work ethic, and so on are all important components to understanding the real work environment. . . .

I would advise all school leaders to work with the career education professionals (superintendents of career centers) in your region. Too often we avoid each other to gain a competitive edge on the neighboring district. The world needs to work together to solve the problems of the world. Education should never have barriers.

While many schools can point to graduates who have been successful in life, career-based high schools prepare their students to begin careers the day after they graduate, which allows them a head start in using the global skills needed to adjust to the 21st century. This is not a new concept for career centers; they've always been focused on practical skill sets and lifetimes of change.

What makes them successful is their ability to successfully pivot from the old mindset to the new one.

This is not to say that comprehensive high schools need to be turned into vocational high schools; traditional K–12 school systems should be dedicated to doing what they have always done: preparing their graduates for the next step of their life journey, whether it is in a 4-year university, a 2-year community college, a trade school, the military, or the workforce. But career centers and vocational high schools have had a clear vision, an ability to adapt, and a commitment to giving their graduates the global skills they need. They are responsible for some of the finest success stories of American education, and their flexible philosophy will allow them to continue to pivot through future disruptions.

A 1977 graduate of the Tri-County Career Center in Ohio epitomizes the successful journey of a skills-oriented worker who is also a lifelong learner—the traits we need to instill in all graduates today. Aleta Eberett Adams graduated with a cosmetology degree, served in the U.S. Army, got a bachelor's degree in business, and took a job in Huntsville, Alabama, as a telemetry team member working with rockets. Today, she is the target test director for the Space and Missile Defense Command. She overcame a childhood of poverty with the training and skill set she received in high school. As she says,

> Today . . . I launch some of the largest rockets in the world. Being president of the 1977 senior cosmetology class taught me leadership, graduating with my class showed me I can do anything I put my mind to, and knowing how to cut hair afforded me opportunities to meet people I would have never had the chance to meet. (Adams)

While Adams began her journey in the 20th century, she reinforces for us the importance of acquiring the proper skill set in today's K–12 schooling to thrive in a world that is being disrupted at record paces. Our graduates need skills, grit, and the ability to adjust to a lifetime of change. Adams probably never imagined she would be launching massive rockets.

Try to imagine the future. What can we do today to help our students prepare for it?

Tips for Leading Schools to Global Readiness

⚡ Expose your students to other cultures in the world.

⚡ Give your students the skills to adapt in a lifetime in which learning never stops.

⚡ Do more than prepare students for the future; they are part of the global community today.

⚡ Take a comprehensive approach.

⚡ Make teacher training in global readiness a priority.

⚡ Keep, or add, international languages in schools.

⚡ Reach out to new partners to help your school become global ready.

⚡ Make the program affordable and sustainable.

⚡ Connect your American students with other students in the world.

⚡ Bring in guest speakers.

⚡ Promote opportunities for students to travel abroad or at least explore other countries and cultures virtually.

⚡ Use the Internet to expose students to world events in real time.

⚡ Create core values of inquiry, research, collaboration, presentation, reflection, and a powerful ethic of care.

⚡ Create a deep learning culture to develop people who want to learn for the rest of their lives.

⚡ Allow students to pursue their own interests.

⚡ Lifelong learning is no longer optional.

⚡ Know which global skills you are going to teach and how you are going to teach them and assess them.

Chapter 7 Scenarios for Applying the CAT Strategy

Scenario 1: A teacher approaches his principal and says he would like to implement more future-ready skills in his teaching but he is unsure how to do it. He says he feels there is so much pressure to teach the standards to prepare students for the state test that he is reluctant to deviate too much from the structure that has worked in the past. He asks the principal for ideas. The principal says he will do a classroom walk-through and then make suggestions.

> **Cope:** The principal conducts a walk-through of the teacher's class and sees the students working in pairs and small groups. They have been assigned a topic by the teacher and are researching it on a Chromebook. They will then create a Google Slides presentation and show it to the class.

> **Adjust:** In the days after the walk-through, the principal meets with the teacher for a post conference, and he tells the teacher he is already effectively teaching some future-ready skills when he has the students collaborate, create slides, and give a presentation. He suggests the teacher get more students into the Google suite so the students can share ideas and artifacts online. The principal also recommends the teacher incorporate more project-based learning in his teaching and go online to research global-ready skill sites, including TED Talks on YouTube. The principal encourages the teacher to use his Twitter account to seek out other teachers who are implementing global-ready skills.

> **Transform:** In the months after the post conference, the principal continues to meet with the teacher, and the principal helps the teacher chart how many times he is implementing each skill, how to check the students for understanding, and tips for creating steps to finish the year. The principal encourages the teacher to stay in contact with external experts he discovered on Twitter, and the principal asks the teacher to share his journey with the rest of the staff when school resumes at the beginning of the next school year. He encourages the teacher to continue to take bold, research-based steps and to learn from his mistakes.

The principal encourages the teacher to treat the next year as a critical growth year in which global-ready skills are stressed from the first day of school and to continue to research the skills since they are constantly morphing.

Scenario 2: A group of parents tells the principal at the September PTO meeting that they would like to see some sort of senior project implemented in the curriculum. Though the test scores have been outstanding and the school has a very high rating in the state's accountability system, the parents have heard of other schools that have successfully implemented senior projects and they would like for their high school staff to consider it.

Cope: The principal consults with her school leadership team and district curriculum director. The senior project idea is not a new one, and it has recently been discussed as a viable option for the school as a way to increase rigor. The principal leads the group through some guidelines, and the group agrees to recruit a small number of seniors to pilot a senior project initiative that year.

Adjust: A few weeks later, 12 seniors have been recruited to be a part of the first senior project group, and they are told of the guidelines. They are told they will be researching a topic of their choice, taking a unique angle on it, and writing a paper or creating some sort of project that will be presented to a group of parents and business leaders. The principal uses the school Twitter account to congratulate the group, and she sets future meeting dates with the students.

Transform: In the following months, the principal and teachers assist the students as they complete the projects and present their work to guest panels. The principal and leadership team suggest a senior project course be implemented the following year so students can receive elective credit for their work and have daily support from a teacher. Also, the group recommends that the course be studied in the following year and possibly be made a graduation requirement.

ACTIVITIES TO LEAD SCHOOLS TO GLOBAL READINESS

1. What courses/programs/initiatives do you have in your school to promote global readiness? What will you add? When?

COURSES/ PROGRAMS/ INITIATIVES ALREADY PRESENT	COURSES/ PROGRAMS/ INITIATIVES TO BE ADDED	TIMELINE FOR IMPLEMENTATION

2. Which global skills are currently stressed the most in your school? Which ones do you need to add?

CURRENT GLOBAL SKILLS	GLOBAL SKILLS TO BE ADDED	TIMELINE AND METHOD OF IMPLEMENTATION

3. How will you model the use of global skills in professional development?

4. How can you work with teachers to find great examples of global skills already being used in the curriculum?

5. How can you celebrate the use of global skills by students?

Learn From the Past

Study your actions from the past. Use the following chart to reflect on ways to help your school be a more global-ready campus. Feel free to work through this process with multiple initiatives to look for patterns and clues for future success.

PROMPTS FOR UNDERSTANDING	THE INITIATIVE
List a global-readiness initiative that had a major impact on your school and culture.	
How did you help your staff cope or evaluate progress in the days immediately following the start of the initiative?	
How did you adjust your practices or policies in the weeks after the start of the initiative to make it more successful?	
How did you transform your philosophy or your staff's philosophy to better implement future global-readiness initiatives?	
Looking back, what went well?	
What could have gone better?	
Is there anything else you or your staff learned by going through the event?	
Do you think you and your staff are better prepared to deal with future global-readiness initiatives? Why or why not?	

Diversity

New Challenges in
the School Melting Pot

Give me your tired, your poor,

Your huddled masses yearning to breathe free,

The wretched refuse of your teeming shore.

Send these, the homeless, tempest-tost to me,

I lift my lamp beside the golden door!

> —Quote at the base of the Statue of Liberty, 1903

Students are hearing more hate language than I have ever heard at our school before.

> —High School Teacher, Helena, Montana, 2016

America's neighborhood schools mirror American society: They are the melting pot of American society. What you see in America, you see in its schools.

And that's why so many educators signed up to be educators: to help young people from all kinds of backgrounds, from different religions, from different cultures and countries, from rich and poor households, to be successful. When administrators crossed that career line between the classroom and the school office for the first time and became administrators, they took a quiet oath to shoulder more responsibility in their mission. They remain committed today to helping students, teachers, parents, and community members find their place in our public schools. This is one of our greatest and most necessary disruptions.

But it's never been more difficult.

It used to be that the greatest diversity challenges in American schools concerned racial issues; schools often struggled with racial tension as black and Latino students began to enroll in predominantly white schools. Of course, diversity in schools today is more than racial diversity; this disruption has added more layers of responsibility and worry—and possibility—for American administrators. School leaders today must help students from different economic backgrounds, students who are LGBTQ, students with different religions, Gen Z students with widely different voices and opinions, students who struggle with gender inequality, students with disabilities, and any other student whose voice dares to be different. Principals and superintendents are helping more students than ever before; yet school leaders struggle to find answers to persistent diversity questions that have plagued American schools, and American society, since their inception and new ones that have arrived at our doorstep with the dawning of the Information Age.

- How do we protect the rights of all students and maintain a stable education environment when there are more attacks on multicultural ideals?

- Should we help our students assimilate or maintain their own, distinct cultures?

- How can we ensure that students in schools with impoverished enrollments have the same opportunities as more affluent students in other schools?

- How do we help our largest minority groups, our black and Latino students, be more successful?

- How do we assist our LGBTQ students and quickly implement the mandates of court decisions or presidential directives?

- How can we get more females into male-dominated courses and ensure that gender equality is a strong part of the school culture?

- Where is the line in schools between freedom of religion and its infringement on the rights of others?

- How do we diversify our teaching force so it more closely mirrors our student diversity?

And now we have a president in Donald Trump who, for right or for wrong reasons, has made immigration reform and border security one of his biggest goals. This has raised tensions in society and in American schools, with their growing immigrant populations—and placed American school leaders in an even more difficult position as they try to dignify all sides, listen to all voices, and continue to educate young people.

Principals and superintendents know ethically they want to be part of the solution and not part of the problem—and they also know any missteps could land them in the lead story of the local news and prompt students to exit their schools for the growing number of charter schools, online schools, or homeschooling options.

The complexity of this diversity will not abate anytime soon. As American schools become even more diverse, the needs of their student populations will grow and school leaders will need to do even more. The questions posed above are essential parts of the American school fabric, but within the American leadership community, a greater question is looming: How do we help our school leaders survive all this?

AN OPEN-DOOR POLICY

First and foremost, American schools pride themselves on welcoming all immigrants. Regardless of the challenge, schools find room and get the students into classes, and teachers start educating them. A recent article in *The Washington Post* highlighted the challenges found in American schools when helping immigrant or displaced students:

> *Many of the new arrivals don't speak much English and are behind academically. They often come with scars, having fled desperate poverty or violence or both. Many endured difficult journeys, sometimes leaving their families behind*

or rejoining parents in the United States after years of separation. And U.S. schools, already strapped for resources, are trying to provide special services, including English-language instruction and mental-health care.

The schools have to, because it's the law: Children who are living in this country have a right to a public education, regardless of their immigration status. But for many educators it's also more than a legal obligation, it's the moral thing to do.

"The United States is founded on human rights," said Sandra Jimenez, the principal of High Point High School in Prince George's County, Md., a Washington suburb where the immigrant population has grown rapidly. "The only reason these people are here is because they are desperate. These people are coming to survive." (Brown, "As Immigration Resurges")

Principal Jimenez speaks for all American administrators: "These people are coming to survive." And the leaders want to help them, even as they deal with the many other disruptions in the schools that vie for administrators' time and energy.

THE GROWTH OF ETHNIC DIVERSITY IN AMERICAN SCHOOLS

Education Week reported in October 2016 that American schools had hit a new diversity milestone: For the first time, the majority of enrolled students would be from minority groups.

The new collective majority of minority schoolchildren—projected to be 50.3 percent by the National Center for Education Statistics—is driven largely by dramatic growth in the Latino population and a decline in the white population, and, to a lesser degree, by a steady rise in the number of Asian-Americans. African-American growth has been mostly flat.

That new majority will continue to grow, the same projections show.

It's a shift that poses a plain imperative for public schools and society at large, demographers and educators say: The United States must vastly improve the educational outcomes for this new and diverse majority of American students, whose success is inextricably linked to the well-being of the nation. (Maxwell)

American educator leaders have a new challenge: finding ways to shift resources to help this population as more and more disruptions enter American schools.

WELCOMING DIVERSITY: A MELTING POT OR A MOSAIC?

At times American school leaders receive mixed messages about helping immigrants in their schools. Is our mission to help the students assimilate into American culture, or are we to strongly help them maintain their cultural identity as they become educated? Or is it a mixture of both? An article in *Education Leadership* from over 20 years ago addressed this quandary.

In recent years, many educators have supported multicultural education as a way to deal with global interconnectedness and America's increasingly multiethnic population. What is disconcerting is that educators have yet to agree on what multiculturalism really is or how it might affect curriculum and teaching. . . . Indeed, two different—and diametrically opposed—perspectives of multiculturalism are currently vying for predominance. The goal of cultural pluralism is that ethnic groups will remain intact and that their idiosyncratic ways of knowing and acting will be respected and continued. Assimilationism, on the other hand, accepts the importance of understanding multiple beliefs, but has as its primary goal the amalgamation of all groups into the American mainstream. (Janzen)

As schools grow more diverse, school leaders will have to spend more time than ever listening, guiding, and working to ensure their newest students have found their place in the school culture—and that place might vary from group to group and family to family depending on the views of the students and the parents.

LEADING IN A CLIMATE OF FEAR

The current political climate that began with the election of 2016 compounds everything for students, teachers, administrators, and parents. Anecdotal stories from experienced educators about the shift in school climates can be heard across America, and a survey released by the Southern Poverty Law Center and cited by the National Education Association during the campaign season provides some hard evidence about how the vitriolic language of American politics is seeping into the school hallways and classrooms:

> *Through an online survey, 2,000 K–12 educators answered questions about what they are seeing at their schools. Nearly 70 percent of those educators said students have expressed concerns about what might happen to their families after the November election, stating that most of those students are immigrants, children of immigrants, and Muslims. More than half of the teachers surveyed have seen an increase in hateful language, with more than a third seeing an increase specifically in anti-Muslim or anti-immigrant speech. . . .*
>
> *Students are suffering panic attacks, fearful for their well-being and that of their family, and some no longer want to come to school because they believe that their classmates hate them. Other students, including some who aren't being targeted, are confused and upset by the rhetoric they hear from presidential candidates and their classmates that conflicts with the American ideals of acceptance and freedom they have learned about at school.* (Litvinov)

It's often the administrator's voice that must be heard. In dark times, it must be a ray of light that others may follow. Now more than ever, administrators must be visible and plugged in with their students and staff.

Besides being concerned for the students, think of how this must be impacting educators. They became teachers and administrators to help students, and now they are dealing with chants about walls, deportation threats in elementary schools, student panic attacks, and confusion—as they try to stress the American ideals of acceptance and freedom. Students, parents, and teachers look to the administrators to lead them through these issues; the stakes are enormous and the stress levels are extremely high. Some of the cuts into the souls of American school leaders in this period of our history will be very deep.

One can look to Eden Prairie, Minnesota, for an example of the consequences that can come with managing diversity. In 2010 the school district created an initiative to redraw school boundary lines to more equitably distribute low-income and minority students in an attempt to close achievement gaps.

> *What followed was a wrenching series of public meetings, protests and online organizing campaigns whose ferocity shocked many longtime residents. In the end, the controversy upended the school board and prompted about two dozen administrators to flee the district, including Eden Prairie's long-serving superintendent.* (Toppo and Overberg)

To repeat, 24 administrators, including the superintendent, eventually left the district. Today, dealing with online organizing, moderating wrenching meetings, and withstanding ferocity can quickly become part of the culture—and job description—for school administrators.

RESEGREGATION: A GROWING RACIAL AND POVERTY GAP

Many of our poorest schools are being challenged by economics, racial isolation, and a lack of opportunities for their young people. While *Brown v. Board of Education* was supposed to equalize the education field for all students in 1954, our most impoverished students, including many black and Hispanic students, have been left behind as other more economically advantaged students have moved into the suburbs or more affluent areas. It's also important to note that Hispanics now "constitute the largest minority group in the United States and the fastest growing segment of its school-age population" (Gandara). A 2016 article in *The Washington Post* highlighted the problem of resegregated American schools for many of our black and Hispanic students:

Poor, black and Hispanic children are becoming increasingly isolated from their white, affluent peers in the nation's public schools, according to new federal data showing that the number of high-poverty schools serving primarily black and brown students more than doubled between 2001 and 2014.

The data was released by the Government Accountability Office . . . 62 years to the day after the Supreme Court decided that segregated schools are "inherently unequal" and therefore unconstitutional.

That landmark decision in Brown v. Board of Education began the dismantling of the dual school systems—one for white kids, one for black students—that characterized so many of the nation's communities. It also became a touchstone for the ideal of public education as a great equalizer, an American birthright meant to give every child a fair shot at success. (Brown, "On the Anniversary of Brown v. Board")

But the *Brown v. Board of Education* decision has not achieved all its desired results. Many of these students attend schools in the inner cities that were once in vibrant middle-class neighborhoods, but the schools have been disrupted through the decades as the demographics shifted. Now administrators in these schools must try to overcome myriad problems. Today, 16% of American schools whose enrollment is made up mainly of students of color represent 61% of all high-poverty schools (Camera). This creates serious obstacles for the children in those schools, their teachers and administrators, and American society.

Mountains of research show that desegregated schools are linked to important benefits, like prejudice reduction, heightened civic engagement and analytical thinking, and better learning outcomes in general.

"When kids are exposed to children who are different than them, whether it's along racial lines or economic lines, that contact between different groups reduces the willingness of kids to make stereotypes and generalizations about other groups," says Genevieve Siegel-Hawley, assistant professor at Virginia Commonwealth University School of Education. "It also reduces anxiety because a lot of prejudice grows

out of fear of the unknown and feeling anxious when you're around different people because you've never had that experience before." (Camera)

These schools are often filled with outstanding educators. The administrators in them must deal with many of the problems associated with educating young people, but they must do it within the context of extreme poverty, violent neighborhoods with high crime rates, and parents who often don't have the education level or resources to support their children. They must be resourceful and develop tight relationships with parents and teachers to form a strong, unified team.

These are some of the toughest leadership roles in all of American education. One leader who has stepped into this void is Todd A. Walker, PhD, the director of the Columbus Africentric Early College P–12 in Columbus, Ohio.

Stories From Exceptional Educational Leaders

Dr. Todd A. Walker, Director
Columbus Africentric Early College P-12
Columbus, Ohio

I believe the greatest challenge that urban school leaders face is to creatively confront the persistent deficit narrative that pervades so many sectors of our society as it relates to urban youth. These young people are brilliant, creative, and passionate, with no less potential or ability to achieve and contribute to our society than other young persons not similarly situated; their voice is critically important at this juncture in our nation's history. In my work as an urban school leader I continually work with colleagues to challenge mindsets and structures that hinder the development of students' capacity. This means focusing inward, inspecting our pedagogical practices to ensure that we are maximizing every teaching moment, and reaching outward, expanding networks of support and available resources to remove learning boundaries.

(Continued)

(Continued)

In many ways, the challenges that our students face, whether in urban, suburban, or rural contexts, are the same. Each student, to achieve success, requires at least one caring adult with high expectations and rigorous instruction. The difference is in where these sources of inspiration and guidance are located. The network of support for most suburban youth is expansive, often located across a diversity of accessible resources in their community, while for many urban and rural youth, there is frequently a lack of accessibility. Therefore, at least some of these networks must be supplemented to ensure student success.

We are a campus for ALL students. Our vision is high achievement and early college for each student as we affirm the positive leadership of African Americans to benefit the global community. Our mission is to provide a high expectation, high support, accelerated learning environment and to serve as an extension center for African and African American cultural learning in the broader Columbus community. Grounded in rigorous academic development of traditional reading, writing, math, social studies, and science skills, our curriculum also develops student confidence. As they explore the cultures and contributions of African peoples and African Americans, students develop a deeply rooted sense of human worth, an appreciation of influences from the African diaspora and connection to the greater global community.

Parents today can also choose to educate their children in charter schools, online, or at home. Columbus City Schools and a number of other urban districts have attempted to be more competitive, with new types of schools built around themes or careers, as in Walker's Africentric Early College.

Competition in the modern era of schooling is broad and far-reaching. Students can choose from a wide variety of programming options available in public, private, and charter schools. This type of competition makes it imperative that school leaders think with clarity about their organizations' specific marketplace niches. I have found it important in my leadership roles to be able to answer questions regarding branding, core values, mission, and vision to communicate program significance to prospective students and families. My frame for competition in contemporary education is that it is not "new" but has shifted. The difference today is that competition is no longer solely associated with neighborhood location but extends across regions via school choice. This necessitates that educators think differently about how they attract and retain students.

Due to increasing choice and selectivity in the education sector, thriving urban schools will likely continue to become progressively specialized in their program offerings. The demand of an expanding choice marketplace also necessitates improved brand articulation and the need to develop and utilize communication platforms that make clear connections between family/student needs and school program offerings.

In the future "competition" will look much like it does today but will become increasingly ubiquitous. Schools' ability to develop instructional capacity tailored for their community contexts and then market to parents with an increased awareness of metrics for educational success will be the barometer of fitness in this environment.

Walker mentions an important point about urban schools that could be applicable to other schools: School leaders will have to work harder to establish a unique brand, culture, and set of outcomes.

All public school leaders know the days of having a monopoly on the school business are over. Consider this data about charter schools from the National Center for Education Statistics:

- Between 2003 and 2014, the percentage of all public schools that were public charter schools increased from 3.1% to 6.6%. The actual number of schools increased from 3,000 to 6,500.

- Charter schools have also increased enrollment in that time frame: The percentage of students with between 300 and 1,000 students increased, while the number of schools with fewer than 300 students went down ("Fast Facts").

Furthermore, a study by the National Center for Education Statistics about homeschooling in 2012 found that about 3% of American students were homeschooled; the main reason for choosing to homeschool children was concern about school environments ("Homeschooling").

Whether they lead an urban, suburban, or rural school, today's school leaders must be looking around to see the latest version of a school down the street that might offer their students something the students are not getting in their current school. School leaders believe in their schools and they hate to see students make a choice to leave—and they also know the students, depending on the state regulations, will probably be taking their allocated state funding with them to the new school, which means the administrator is seeing thousands of dollars in funding walking out the door. The more students lost, the greater the budget reduction, which will inevitably have a negative impact on overall educational programming.

RACIAL DIVERSITY IN MIDDLE AMERICA

Working through issues in ethnic diversity is not confined to urban or suburban schools. School leaders in relatively homogeneous communities must also work diligently to help their students understand the benefits of diversity. One leader who understands this is award-winning superintendent of schools Steve Woolf, of USD 101 Erie-Galesburg in Erie, Kansas.

Stories From Exceptional Educational Leaders

Steve Woolf, Superintendent

USD 101 Erie-Galesburg

Erie, Kansas

While the great population centers, and where most of the nation's population reside, have quite a bit of diversity in their population, the majority of the nation as it pertains to area has very little diversity. The challenge I have is to prepare our students and staffulty to know how to relate to anyone other than people who are just like them.

The population in our school district is like most of the school districts in Kansas—94% white, middle class to poverty, with 6% other being mostly students of Hispanic descent or African American. We are starting to see a migration of students whose parents are first generation in this nation, do not speak English, and are primarily of Hispanic descent. This is happening in schools where pickups (the majority of the vehicles our kids drive) sit out in our parking lots with Confederate flag license plates and decals to go with their Trump stickers. This is being reinforced in our homes by parents who continually vote against their own best interests, and when they see someone different than themselves show up, they finally have someone right there they can blame and cut down. Frankly, our kids are better than the adults by a long shot, but it is hard to take what they have heard at home their whole life and show them the amazing gift of diversity and building relationships with others who are different than you.

I say all this with a scene clearly in my mind where the former mayor of our city, a man in his 70s, greets me as we enter a basketball tournament in a neighboring city with, "Hey, there! How's the HNIC!" I was dumbfounded. . . . Frankly, I feel things will improve as this older generation who grew up as closet racists fade away from this earth.

I am in my 30th year as an educator—4 as a teacher, 18 as a principal, and 8 as a superintendent. We are both better and worse than we have ever been dealing with diversity, from the time I started in education to today. So many more cultures have risen that we knew nothing about when I started. To be frank, one of the major issues I am dealing with right now as a superintendent is educating my school board on the law, their responsibility, and what they can and can't do as a board member dealing with issues of diversity that arise. . . .

I LOVE that our students are embracing diversity in this mono-cultural environment. We'll drag the adults along kicking and screaming for the most part.

Superintendent Woolf brings up a point often heard from school leaders: It's not the students who are the most difficult in dealing with diversity; it's the adults.

SCHOOLS: TO PRAY OR NOT TO PRAY

Consider some of the religious controversies in America's schools from the past decade:

- A high school principal in North Texas discusses his religious beliefs with a group of students at a prayer meeting one morning before school, and it sets off a flurry of complaints and counter-complaints from students and parents.

- A middle school principal in New York asks a student to omit references to religion from a speech and is sued.

- An elementary school in Kansas comes under attack for having a bulletin board in its school that features the five pillars of Islam.

It's never been easy to lead through religious controversies in schools. Now every school leader's decision can be broadcast via the mainstream media and through social media. The confluence of cultures and religions in schools makes religious issues more complex than ever before. A 2007 report from the Pew Research Center still summarizes the difficulty faced by American school leaders when confronting religion questions:

Nearly a half-century after the Supreme Court issued its landmark ruling striking down school-sponsored prayer, Americans continue to fight over the place of religion in public schools. Indeed, the classroom has become one of the most important battlegrounds in the broader conflict over religion's role in public life. . . .

Some Americans are troubled by what they see as an effort on the part of federal courts and civil liberties advocates to exclude God and religious sentiment from public schools. Such an effort, these Americans believe, infringes upon the First Amendment right to the free exercise of religion.

Civil libertarians and others, meanwhile, voice concern that conservative Christians are trying to impose their values on students of all religious stripes. Federal courts, the civil libertarians point out, have consistently interpreted the First Amendment's prohibition on the establishment of religion to forbid state sponsorship of prayer and most other religious activities in public schools. (Liu)

To summarize, some Americans are troubled by efforts to exclude God from public schools—while others are concerned that conservative Christians, and perhaps more groups today, are gaining too much of a presence in public schools.

Many school leaders have seen this same scenario in their schools. They can hear from one parent about a religious opinion and from another parent 10 minutes later who takes the opposite view. Religion is one of the most hotly debated, and fought over, topics in American schools. Now more than ever, school leaders must balance how to foster independent thinking in students with what is legal, and weigh it all with the opinion of the community. That's a difficult task in an era of widespread disruptions. There are often no clear answers.

PROTECTING GAY RIGHTS: TO HELP STUDENTS WALKING THROUGH A HAILSTORM

In late 2016, Human Rights Watch released a report on the experiences of LGBT youth in American schools. The report is titled *"Like Walking Through a Hailstorm,"* which is what one parent of an LGBT student said it was like for her child each day in school.

The report had these recommendations for school administrators.

Recommendations for Protecting the Rights and Health of LGBT Students

- *Ensure that school policies against bullying and harassment include enumerated protections on the basis of sexual orientation and gender identity;*

- *Ensure that the school provides comprehensive sexuality education that is inclusive of LGBT youth, covers same-sex activity on equal footing with other sexual activity, and is medically and scientifically accurate;*

- *Ensure that GSAs and other LGBT student organizations are permitted to form and operate on the same terms as all other student organizations;*

- *Ensure that same-sex couples are able to date, display affection, and attend dances and other school functions on the same terms as all other student couples;*

- *Ensure that students are able to access facilities, express themselves, and participate in classes, sports teams, and extracurricular activities in accordance with their gender identity.* ("Like Walking Through a Hailstorm")

Many administrators already use these guidelines, while others do not, either because they haven't encountered some of these situations yet or they are in states where LGBT rules are not recognized. According to the report, some states (Alabama, Arizona, Louisiana, Mississippi, Oklahoma, South Carolina, Texas, and Utah) have laws that restrict staff members from discussing LGBT issues in schools.

While administrators can be advocates for change, they often work within the tight cultural and legal confinements of their communities and states. They must navigate through the barriers set by others as they try to help their students. In many schools, LGBT rights are much more accepted than in the past, but school administrators often find themselves on the front lines as more battles are waged; it is one of the most publicly viewed disruptions in which administrators find themselves.

RESTROOMS: BOYS, GIRLS, AND GENDERLESS

Many administrators never thought they would be wondering how to create genderless restrooms. But this disruption was suddenly thrust into their operations in May 2016 when the White House issued its directive to allow transgender students to use the bathroom that matches their gender identity. To receive federal funds, the directive stated, "a school may provide separate facilities on the basis of sex, but must allow transgender students access to such facilities consistent with their gender identity." Furthermore, schools were not allowed to demand any sort of documentation from the students about their gender identity (Dooley).

Many of today's administrators would gladly help their transgender students, but the problem is usually the need to suddenly designate some restrooms as genderless in buildings where all the current boys' and girls' restrooms are already labeled and frequently used.

Plus, there are some instances when the school leaders find themselves in the middle of lawsuits pertaining to the issue. The school board of Gloucester County in Virginia filed a suit to overturn a lower court's ruling that one of the district's students, Gavin Grimm, should be allowed to use the restroom of his choice. Consider some of the quotes from an article about this case.

"It means I'm going to have to spend another school year where I should be focused on college plans and prom and graduation . . . not able to use the bathroom at my school," Grimm said. . . .

"We're prepared to make our case to the court and to make sure the Supreme Court and people in general see Gavin as who he is and see trans kids across the country for who they are," said Grimm's attorney, Joshua Block of the American Civil Liberties Union. Grimm "is not trying to dismantle sex-segregated restrooms. He's just trying to use them."

Troy Andersen, chairman of the Gloucester County School Board, said in a statement that the board is "grateful that the Supreme Court has granted the School Board's petition in this difficult case." (Barnes and Balingit)

Imagine the bundle of emotions felt by everyone in this case, and in similar ones as they play out across the country. School leaders are now in an era when the rights of the individual, including those with previously unrecognized rights, are to be immediately recognized. This is not to say the rights are right or wrong. It is often *not* the place of the administrator to render judgment—the judgments are often brought from the school boards and courts—but it is the school leader's job to implement the changes and lead the staff, students, and community through the adjustments and keep people focused on educating the young people.

TRYING TO DIVERSIFY THE TEACHING FORCE

American schools address diversity disruptions today while still struggling with one of the oldest ones: the need to provide high-quality teachers of all backgrounds in the teaching force. A report released by the Albert Shanker Institute in 2015 summarized how minority students and others benefit from a diverse teaching staff:

- *Minority teachers can be more motivated to work with disadvantaged minority students in high-poverty, racially and ethnically segregated schools, a factor which may help to reduce rates of teacher attrition in hard-to-staff schools.*

- *Minority teachers tend to have higher academic expectations for minority students, which can result in increased academic and social growth among students.*

- *Minority students profit from having among their teachers individuals from their own racial and ethnic group who can serve as academically successful role models and who can have greater knowledge of their heritage culture.*

- *Positive exposure to individuals from a variety of races and ethnic groups, especially in childhood, can help to reduce stereotypes, attenuate unconscious implicit biases and help promote cross-cultural social bonding.*

- *All students benefit from being educated by teachers from a variety of different backgrounds, races and ethnic groups.* (Albert Shanker Institute)

The growing diversity of our enrollments in ethnicity, cultural background, sexual preference, sexual identity, and immigrant status reinforces a need to take an even broader look at the diversity needed in the teaching force. For American K–12 education to reach its full potential, American school leaders should continue to search for ways to have their staff match the diversity of the American population.

Tips for Leading Schools in Diversity Disruptions

⚡ As schools grow more diverse, school leaders will have to spend more time than ever listening, guiding, and working to ensure their newest students have found their place in the school culture.

⚡ In a climate of fear and anger, the administrator's voice must be heard. In dark times, it must be a ray of light that others may follow. Now more than ever, administrators must be visible and plugged in with their students and staff.

⚡ The administrators in impoverished schools must deal with many of the problems associated with educating young people, but they must do it within the context of extreme poverty, violent neighborhoods with high crime rates, and parents who often don't have the education level or resources to support their children. They must be resourceful and develop tight relationships with parents and teachers to form a strong, unified team.

⚡ In the future, many schools will be progressively specialized in their program offerings. School leaders will have to work harder to establish a unique brand, culture, and set of outcomes.

⚡ Diversity efforts are not needed only in places of high diversity; they are just as important in the many parts of America with low levels of minority students. School leaders must prepare students to relate to others who are different from them.

⚡ The confluence of cultures and religions in schools makes religious issues more complex than ever before. School leaders must balance what is right for students with what is legal, and weigh it all with the opinion of the community.

⚡ Know the laws of your state with regard to LGBTQ issues in schools. Be prepared to fight for the rights of your students.

⚡ Be prepared for sudden changes in guidelines, as occurred with the transgender restroom issue. Flexibility is a key to surviving in an age of disruption.

⚡ Administrators have often tried to have staff diversity that is similar to that of the students. With the growing diversity in American students, administrators need to expand their definitions of staff diversity.

Chapter 8 Scenarios for Applying the CAT Strategy

Scenario 1: Two days after a heated national election in which a winning candidate made numerous comments about halting immigration, an American-born student pulls a hijab off the head of a female Somali student who has immigrated with her family to America. In the Somali culture, this act is considered a huge transgression. The student who grabbed the hijab is counseled and punished, and the parents of the girl are notified of what has happened. The next day, the girl's father comes to the school with several other Somali parents, and they want to be reassured the school is a safe place for their children.

Cope: The principal reassures the parents that the administration and staff will do all they can to make the school safe for their students. The principal listens to all concerns and discusses some additional steps that will be taken to increase cultural sensitivity in the school as tensions mount nationally.

Adjust: In the days and weeks after the meeting, the principal confers with students, teachers, and key parents to discuss what has happened and to take advice. The administrators speak in classrooms, club meetings, and across all parts of the student body to calm nerves, assure all students they are welcomed, and tell them what to do if they encounter xenophobic comments or actions. When the administration hears of certain times or places in the school where improper actions are occurring, it focuses on those areas to become more visible and proactive. It also stresses to all stakeholders the positive things occurring in the school and uses social media to share images and videos that support the mission of the school. The administration also works closely with the student who committed the offense to ensure the student has made the event a learning experience.

Transform: In the months after the event, the principal continues to dialogue with stakeholders, to listen, and to adjust strategies. An effort is made to bring in more guest speakers who discuss diversity, and students begin a club that focuses on helping all students be accepted. The administration has been tracking data in its discipline system to monitor the number of reported offenses, and the administrative team informally keeps track of issues by constantly conferring on what it is seeing and hearing. The principal has been meeting with stakeholder groups and is adjusting plans for the next school year and seeking ways to expand diversity training for students and staff.

Scenario 2: A decree is issued from the White House on a Thursday that on the following Monday all LGBTQ students are to have access to the restrooms in which they feel most comfortable. The principal is immediately inundated with questions and comments from students, staff members, and key community stakeholders who have various opinions on the subject. Some are applauding the decree, and some of them are opposed to it. The principal hears both sides use civil rights, religion, and tradition as reasons for being for or against the decree.

Cope: The principal gathers his administrative team and teacher leaders to decide how they will address the issue of allowing students to choose restrooms. The principal stresses to the team and to all stakeholders that they will follow the decree. They decide to reassure LGBTQ students they can use any restroom, and they make immediate plans to consult with student leaders and any LGBTQ students who wish to be a part of the process for moving forward. When the principal meets with students, the principal is advised it could be a good idea to keep most restrooms separated by gender but to have one restroom designated as nongender for any students who are either LGBTQ or non-LGBTQ to use. The principal then meets with the staff to keep them informed of what is happening, to listen to ideas, and to remind them the world is changing rapidly and schools must constantly adjust. The principal uses social media to inform the public of what is happening. Student leaders and teachers also use social media to share their ideas.

(Continued)

(Continued)

Adjust: In the weeks after the decree is implemented, the principal notices the community uproar has subsided. The staff deals with several homophobic statements made by some students, but for the most part the students are adjusting well to the new rules about restroom use. The principal stays in contact with parent leaders, monitors social media content, and remains in close contact with LGBTQ students and student leaders.

Transform: In the months after the decree, the principal meets with the full staff and asks them to review the entire process and to add comments about what went well, what could be improved, and what was learned. The principal also stays in contact with parent leaders and works with LGBTQ students who wish to form their own advisory council so the principal can hear ideas for moving forward.

ACTIVITIES TO LEAD IN DIVERSITY DISRUPTIONS

1. How can you protect the rights of all students and maintain a stable education environment, especially in this era when there are more attacks on minorities?

2. How will you help your students assimilate and/or maintain their own, distinct cultures?

3. How will you ensure that your impoverished students have the same opportunities as your more affluent students?

4. How will you ensure there are no achievement gaps between ethnic groups in your school?

5. How can you help your LGBTQ students have a safe environment?

6. How will you accommodate the freedom of students to have religious beliefs without allowing it to infringe on the rights of others?

7. How can you diversify your teaching force so it more closely mirrors your student diversity?

Learn From the Past

Study your actions from the past. Use the following chart to reflect on diversity disruptions and what you did to cope, adjust, and transform with them. Read the prompts on the left and fill in the boxes on the right. Feel free to work through this process with multiple disruptive events to look for patterns and clues for future success.

PROMPTS FOR UNDERSTANDING	YOUR DISRUPTIVE EVENT
List a diversity disruptive event that challenged you and your staff.	
How did you help your staff cope in the days immediately following the event?	
How did you adjust your practices or policies in the weeks after the event?	
How did you transform your philosophy or your staff's philosophy to better deal with future diversity disruptions?	
Looking back, what went well?	
What could have gone better?	
Is there anything else you or your staff learned by going through the event?	
Do you think you and your staff are better prepared to deal with future diversity challenges? Why or why not?	

Transparency
The World Is Watching

I think there is a lot of fear in the word transparent, *especially when it comes to the world of education. The trust instilled in you as an educator, administrator, or whatever role you may play is a make or break in my mind and will ultimately lead to your success or failure.*

—Patrick Galloway, Director of Communications for
New Albany-Plain Local Schools

Not only are school leaders dealing with the greatest number of disruptions in school history, they are doing it in the most transparent environment in history. Trust used to be given freely to school administrators; now it must be earned daily—and it can be lost daily. Administrators live with the knowledge that each day can begin well but if a serious event happens during the day, they will be judged not only on how they handled it but on how transparent they were in letting people know what happened, why it happened, what was done about it, and what will be done in the future to prevent it from happening again.

Before the rise of the Internet, and before cable television allowed television news to run in a 24-hour cycle, school transparency consisted of letters about upcoming events sent home to parents, or perhaps an occasional telephone conversation between a teacher and parent that the teacher placed in the teachers' lounge. Teachers who were lucky might have a private room off to the side of the lounge that was reserved for phone calls; these rooms can now be seen as initial efforts by school leaders to encourage calls to parents while maintaining student privacy.

Today, the challenge of maintaining transparency for stakeholders is enormous. There is so much to report, so many ways of doing it, and so much at stake that it can easily become one of the most important functions for administrators.

Look at the new duties that have fallen on administrators within the past 20 years.

- Administrators now have e-mail and voice mail, and it's not unusual for them to find messages that were delivered at 2:00 and 3:00 in the morning. There used to be an 8-hour window for communication during the school day; now it's been expanded to 24 hours. It's a positive development for parents, but it's increased the volume of communication, and administrators are challenged to keep up with it.

- Student information management systems place huge amounts of data in the hands of parents whenever they wish to access it. This could include grades, attendance, grade point averages, and even the amount spent on lunches. This is another positive step for parents, but the administrators are expected to keep the information flowing. Gen Z students can log onto the systems with their phones at the end of the day and see a grade from a test they took that morning; they expect prompt results.

- Parents expect teachers to keep their portals or web pages up-to-date with assignments. If a particular teacher is slow to update a page, then the administrator is expected to intervene.

- It is now an assumption in today's digital world that schools and districts will maintain professional, robust web pages. These can be very expensive, and they are expected to be current.

- Administrators must now scramble to promptly inform parents and the community about any unusual events at school, such as a threat, fight, accident, or disturbance. The school leaders must determine what is worthy of dissemination and what is not. This notification could be a banner on the school web page and then an e-mail sent out by the principal or district office.

Or perhaps the school has invested in an emergency messaging system that sends a rapid flurry of texts and e-mails to multiple recipients: all the cell phones and e-mail accounts of parents, stepparents, grandparents, and anyone on the emergency notification list for each student. If such a system is used and a parent somehow is not notified, then the parent often calls or writes the next day seeking answers.

And through it all, there is the constant hum of social media dissecting the situation.

School leaders accept that these responsibilities are part of their new 21st century job descriptions. But when added to all their other duties—the ones left over from before the age of disruption and the new ones that continue to evolve—it can be overwhelming.

IT'S ABOUT TRUST

As Patrick Galloway, the experienced director of communications for New Albany-Plain Local Schools in New Albany, Ohio, emphasizes in the chapter opening, it's about trust in today's schools, and this can ultimately lead to an administrator's success or failure.

Galloway makes these points for school leaders.

Stories From Exceptional Educational Leaders

Patrick Galloway, Director of Communications
New Albany-Plain Local Schools
New Albany, Ohio

Schools have been much more transparent in the sharing of information with families, students, staff, and the community at large due to a number of factors. Based on my experience there are several resources now at the fingertips of parents, the community, and others that in my opinion make it essential that schools take the time to efficiently and effectively

(Continued)

(Continued)

communicate information to their constituents to ensure accuracy and a thorough account of what it is that schools would like to share and/or promote.

As an example, with the surge in social media, texting, e-mail, and more, students, staff, and parents are sharing information in a rapid manner and delivering an account of something that happened much sooner than sometimes a school can deliver. It is with this knowledge that we owe it to our constituents and the greater community to share what we can to prevent a story from being miscommunicated, taken out of context, or shared with inaccurate or selective details. Putting our best effort into sharing what we can when it is appropriate and with complete details is essential to building trust with our community.

In our current reality, it is imperative for schools to communicate as if anyone is a constituent. The information that you share will impact many—students, staff, community, and families. Simplicity is also a goal to strive for when communicating transparently. A direct message that contains the "need to know" information is so important, especially in an emergency or critical situation.

The media used to be the local newspaper, or perhaps a local television station in larger cities. While those entities are still present, they are now linked via the Internet to other platforms, and any story can be shared well beyond the school district boundaries. Galloway knows the importance of effectively dealing with all kinds of media.

Media relations is a very important component to helping us tell our story as a school district and a learning community. We should view our relationship with our media partners as a positive one and remember to nurture the relationship whenever possible. The hope is that by being open to media and demonstrating our willingness to share information for a given story or talk honestly about the issues facing education, our school or student concerns will lead to future opportunities for positive story placement and pitches from my district. There are times when it can be difficult to assume positive intentions when it comes to media.

Public records requests are sometimes viewed as a way to "discover" what is wrong or bad about a school district or if there are challenges that a district or school is not sharing for various reasons. Again, I always approach these situations with an open mind and will share what we are legally permitted to share regarding the request. I have seen many colleagues shot down though when they feel the media are trying to "make news" rather than covering something for the sake of the greater good, and I think it definitely impacts their relationship at times with the media.

Galloway also knows that transparency can have both positive and negative connotations for parents and the local public.

It establishes a foundation of honesty and leads to the satisfaction that you know you are doing everything you can to operate and communicate without barriers. You feel better about your work, the work of the district, and the quality of instruction and integrity of support to the students. The commitment to transparency also adds clarity to the work of the district by enabling everyone to be focused on the same goals without any hidden agendas or ideas, or practices that are only shared by a few. I believe an additional positive impact is that it is a catalyst for idea sharing and allows people the freedom to share with their colleagues without fear.

Transparency can lead to a few things that can certainly reflect negatively on a district or learning community. Sometimes providing too much information even if you feel it is necessary can convolute or exacerbate a situation. It is always best to focus on the facts and the situation at hand, not drift to other ideas or ramifications or consequences. Information that goes a step further in this way could be relayed in follow-up communications. Also, this can lead to overcommunicating, where you risk the potential of losing your audience altogether. It is not about a lack of transparency, but the details of a situation should be limited to those that are most important.

Check yourself and have others check your messaging. It sounds very simple, but sometimes the perspective from a colleague, another administrator, or possibly even someone outside of the district or your current workplace can help you better understand how a message or your communication could be perceived.

Obviously one of the most direct measures is feedback based on the response to the message. Have you made a situation worse, satisfied a concern, or at least shared all that there was to share at that moment? It is vital that you reflect on the response and reaction to your message and communications so you are listening to your audience and can tailor

(Continued)

(Continued)

it moving forward. It is essential to be open to feedback and to others' opinions and ideas to continue to build that needed trust with your community. If you do not receive feedback, seek it on your own, through survey instruments or even by forming a focus group.

Galloway mentions an interesting new problem for school leaders as they deal with the transparency disruption: overcommunicating, the idea that in our efforts to be transparent we provide so much information that the audience quits listening. Yet if we don't provide enough information, then the public will lose its trust of the school district.

There are often no easy solutions for solving the transparency riddle.

A VIEW OF TRANSPARENCY FROM THE PAST CENTURY TO THE PRESENT

Keith Bell began his career in the 20th century as a teacher, and he finished his public school career as a recognized 21st century superintendent. He now teaches at the Ohio State University. He has seen transparency shifting from the past to the present, and he has seen it from different levels of school leadership.

Stories From Exceptional Educational Leaders

Keith Bell, Instructor
The Ohio State University
Columbus, Ohio

Schools have become more transparent for a couple of reasons. First, they should be! When I started my career it was almost as if good teaching was kept a secret and those individuals who had a unique or specific skill set that could support achievement were not utilized to support those who didn't. I believe it was thought by many if they had the knowledge then they could separate themselves from everyone else and be held in a higher regard (financially and professionally). We have learned since that educating children successfully in the

21st century requires a collaborative effort from all stakeholders and accountability is a team effort and not something that can be completed successfully in a silo.

Second, the millennial movement has forced school districts to look differently at how they communicate. Marketing for education was not something many of us learned as a part of our methodology classes, but it is critical in the success of any organization. As a marketing education/ business education major and teacher of marketing for 14 years, I understood this. I believe districts now understand how important this area is, and the evidence is supported in parents being able to access grades online, track progress online, and so on; there is even an application that will notify parents when a student has not turned in an assignment or has dropped a letter grade in a course. Because many individuals now get news digitally, districts are adjusting and communicating differently to ensure that information is being communicated to all stakeholders in a timely manner. The competition for students with charter and private schools and what I believe is a movement to privatize public education are further reasons why marketing for education is necessary. Many times parents and community stakeholders get pertinent news impacting the school before school officials do, which makes transparency all the more important. . . .

Transparency has been positive for me, as it has helped get stakeholders to the truth. I wasn't smart enough to remember what I could make up, so to me it was easier to just tell the truth and that way I would not need to remember what I said. Sometimes people can't handle the truth. For example, as a head basketball coach, when I cut players I told them to their faces and did not post a list. If I could not tell them negative news face-to-face, I should not share the news. I didn't care how much time it took; they deserved the courtesy of the conversation. For my staff and students, it made it easier for all of them to understand where we were and what we needed to do to improve. Everyone needs to understand and be able to articulate what reality looks like for them. This was my initial rationale behind the state-of-the-school messages, as they gave me an opportunity to communicate directly with staff and students about our collective reality.

Bell knows the media plays a key role in shaping messages for public consumption. He advises leaders to stay ahead of the story and the

(Continued)

(Continued)

media so the public understands what is happening. He stresses the need to be transparent with the media so they will know how to tell the story.

The negative impact has occurred when the media has taken an issue and developed their own rationale or interpretation as to how and why something has occurred, and as a result the district (or I) had to go into "damage control." The negative impact on staff and students is that once the negative message is "out there" it's very difficult to reel things back in. A lack of preparation for a potentially negative message can cost a district and building all the work it took to develop a culture conducive to growing and learning. I have had a number of articles, related to me, my students, or the districts (six) I have served, in our local paper, and thankfully, most of them have been positive.

We have to help the media understand both sides of information. We need to understand that as educators we are not perfect, and therefore, I think acknowledging our shortcomings takes the "teeth out of the dog" with the media. By this I mean if we have already admitted we made a mistake or probably could have done a better job of handling something, they don't have much to write about—especially when you indicate what you learned and your strategies for changing things the next time you are confronted with the same situation. Progress is measured within that accuracy of the message and when there is a mutual understanding between sender and receiver and they can agree on that message.

When you consider that all children in K–12 education now grew up (or are growing up) with computers, social media, and the ability to access information from anywhere at any time, it makes professional sense for district leaders and supporting personnel to gear the education of these stakeholders within an environment that promotes transparency. As I see the impact in the final stages through my current work in higher education (Ohio State), it is even clearer to me how important it is for students to understand the truth through clarity as they continue their academic and professional growth.

A positive theme runs through Bell's comments: Have a philosophy of communicating, build trust, and let the truth come through in your messaging.

ACKNOWLEDGING VULNERABILITY AND SEEKING CLARITY

Michael John Roe, EdD, is the tech-savvy principal of Riverside Poly High School in Riverside, California. He points out the importance of asking key questions and sharing information quickly.

Stories From Exceptional Educational Leaders

Michael John Roe, Principal
Riverside Poly High School
Riverside, California

As we funnel this through the lens of transparency, critical interrogatives need to be asked:

- *What is worth communicating?*
- *Who develops the communication?*
- *How do we ensure that we have measures in place for stakeholders to engage the communication (action orientation)?*
- *How do we use the demand for instant communication to call others to a higher purpose and vision?*
- *How can "transparency" be monitored for effectiveness at all levels?*
- *What structures and systems can we create that will support authentic engagement at all levels?*

I am religious in my use of Twitter, Instagram, and Facebook. Social media can be used to communicate and brand at high levels. Ultimately, we believe that we celebrate what we value—thus the majority of posts that are dedicated to classroom lessons, athletics, and visual and performing arts. We created an immediate social media presence. This gave us a distinct advantage to frame the message, before the message framed us. As a result, the press and select reporters follow my tweets. This has proven advantageous in situations where false information will get circulated throughout

(Continued)

(Continued)

the community. Having a rapid "war room" response is essential to match negative perceptions about your school. The challenge for leadership is who this person or group of people is and how fast they can mobilize.

Roe also stresses the importance of transparency in this age of 24/7 social media. Bad news will eventually be revealed—so he advises leaders to stay ahead of it.

We have learned some things along the way with the use of social media:

- *Don't hide anything.*
- *Volunteer the "negative" news before it gets volunteered for you.*
- *Have students frame the messaging and branding of school.*
- *Create and communicate a social media and communication plan with the community—regularly.*

Roe reminds us of the necessity of Twitter and other social media platforms. Today many parents will first get their news about a school from a principal's or superintendent's Twitter feed if the leaders have systematically developed a stream of news and expanded their number of followers. It can be a powerful tool in both disseminating information and stopping the spread of misinformation.

As social media continues to expand and digitization occurs in schools, more and more information will be available beyond the school walls. School leaders must view transparency as a positive tool that can assist them with their messaging—and that includes using their own smartphones to stay ahead of the story.

Tips for Leading in Transparency Disruptions

⚡ Transparency allows you to get stakeholders to the truth.

⚡ Transparency is a critical part of our branding and will continue to grow in importance in the future.

- Simplicity is also a goal to strive for when communicating. A direct message that contains the "need to know" information is critical, especially in an emergency situation.

- We should view our relationship with our media partners as a positive one and remember to nurture it whenever possible.

- Sometimes providing too much information, even if you feel it is necessary, can convolute or exacerbate a situation. It is always best to focus on the facts and the situation at hand, not drift to other ideas or ramifications or consequences.

- When deciding what to share, ask, "Have I made the situation worse, satisfied a concern, or at least shared all that there was to share at the moment?"

- Develop your social media following to help manage disruptions.

Chapter 9 Scenarios for Applying the CAT Strategy

Scenario 1: A principal is summoned to a men's restroom where a student has found a bomb threat written on the wall of a bathroom stall. The note, written in pen, reads "I'll blow up this school tomorrow!" The threat was seen by a student, who notified his teacher, who notified the principal.

Cope: The principal closes the restroom and calls the police department, who sends a detective to the school to take pictures and start an investigation. The principal notifies the district office and pulls the administrative team together so they can assess the threat level. A school resource officer joins them. The principal asks questions such as, "Is this threat credible? Are there any known bomb makers in the area? Are

(Continued)

there any reports of students experimenting with bombs? Are there any students who had classes near the restroom who could be suspects and can be interviewed? Is there any way to ascertain the time the threat was written?" While the administrative team believes the threat is a hoax, it takes the threat seriously. The principal consults with district office personnel, and they decide to notify the public of what has happened. The principal knows the threat has already been discussed among students, so the principal tells them through the public address system that the school believes the threat is a hoax but they will increase security for the next few days. Students who know anything about the threat are encouraged to come forward to share information. The school sends out an e-mail blast and phone notification to all parents, and the school and district social media platforms are used to reassure parents and students. Security is increased at the school for the next few days.

Adjust: In the weeks after the threat, the principal consults with students, staff, and parents to hear their ideas on how the school handled the situation. The principal reminds all stakeholders to be vigilant and to report any threats of violence immediately to the school or the police. The principal continues to use social media to reassure parents how hard the staff works to provide a safe environment. The student who wrote the threat has not been caught, so the principal reminds custodians and other staff members to be on the alert for future threats.

Transform: In the following months, no more threats have been made, but the principal still asks the staff to reflect on the fact that a student made a threat to blow up the school and what that means for the school's security and learning environment moving forward. The principal reminds the staff that they live in an era of school terrorism and that all threats are taken seriously and the best defense against violence is for all staff members to work together to create a nurturing, transparent environment for all students.

Scenario 2: A principal is informed one night by the superintendent that one of the school's teachers has just been arrested and charged with being in an improper relationship with an underage student. The superintendent says the teacher has been notified not to return to school until more details are learned. The story is covered by all four local news stations the next morning, and they give the name of the teacher with a police photo. Shortly after school begins, all four television stations call the school and leave messages requesting a comment from the principal. They also say they will have camera crews and reporters set up at noon in front of the school to do a live report on the progress of the investigation. The district does not have a school information officer to handle press requests, so it is up to the superintendent and principal to set the public relations course for this crisis.

Cope: During the morning before the press arrives, the principal and superintendent discuss their plan for staying ahead of the story. An assistant principal notifies them that the school hashtag on Twitter is filled with questions and comments from parents and community members. They craft an e-mail that goes out to parents explaining what has happened and assuring them that student safety and teacher professionalism are high priorities. The principal goes on the public address system and tells the students and staff that a teacher has been accused of a crime and it's a serious matter. The principal also reminds them that the accused teacher has not yet been proven guilty and they should all pull together to help each other through this difficult time. The principal also stresses to students and staff the need to focus on trust within the student–teacher relationship and the need to focus on learning and professionalism while the press is focusing on negative behavior. A member of the administration visits each of the accused teacher's classes to answer questions and put them at ease. The student who was in the relationship is not in school, so the principal and guidance counselor contact the student's family to inquire about the student's well-being, to offer emotional support, and to inform the

(Continued)

(Continued)

family about the press requests. The press is requesting that the principal address the public and answer questions during the noon live shoot. The principal and superintendent discuss their options and decide it is better to work with the press and be transparent while protecting the rights of both the student and the accused teacher. At noon, they go out together in front of the school to answer questions from the press. The principal also begins sending out reassuring messages on Twitter and other social media platforms to allay the concerns being found there. At the end of the day, the teacher submits a resignation letter to the district.

Adjust: In the days and weeks after the teacher's arrest and resignation, the principal continues to monitor the story and get updates from the police, and hires a replacement for the teacher. The principal asks the staff to help mitigate rumors and to refer any students who might need counseling to the guidance department. The principal also continues to use social media to reassure students and parents about the safety of the school and the professionalism of the staff. The staff helps the student in the relationship transition back into the school.

Transform: In the months after the event, the principal and superintendent review their response to the event, particularly the sequence of their actions and what they might do differently the next time they are in the middle of a viral story. They review their use of social media and what they could have done differently in their messaging to the community. They consult with other experienced school leaders they have found on Twitter. They also discuss the speed with which the story took off, from the arrest the night before to the impromptu news conference on the school's front lawn 14 hours later. They have learned the necessity of transparency, communication, and speed in dealing with viral school stories in an age of social media and the local press.

ACTIVITIES TO LEAD IN TRANSPARENCY DISRUPTIONS

1. What are the greatest challenges you face with transparency in your school?

2. Where do you and your staff need to improve?

3. Is the school using social media effectively?

4. Are you using social media effectively from your own accounts? Are you increasing your followers?

Learn From the Past

Study your actions from the past. Use the following chart to reflect on transparency disruptions and what you did to cope, adjust, and transform with them. Read the prompts on the left and fill in the boxes on the right. Feel free to work through this process with multiple disruptive events to look for patterns and clues for future success.

PROMPTS FOR UNDERSTANDING	YOUR DISRUPTIVE EVENT
List a transparency disruptive event that challenged you and your staff.	
How did you help your staff cope in the days immediately following the event?	
How did you adjust your practices or policies in the weeks after the event?	
How did you transform your philosophy or your staff's philosophy to better deal with future events?	
Looking back, what went well?	
What could have gone better?	
Is there anything else you or your staff learned by going through the event?	
Do you think you and your staff are better prepared to deal with transparency challenges? Why or why not?	

21st Century School Assessment

More Than Test Scores

It's not about change today and status quo tomorrow—it's about change today, tomorrow, and forever—constant and never ending change—exponential change—there's no more place for investing in the status quo.

—Ian Jukes, Futurist

If we're discussing ways to move America's schools into the 21st century, shouldn't we measure their progress with a 21st century set of standards? As the principals and superintendents who have contributed to this book have pointed out, their goals are no longer centered solely on test scores; they also focus on student safety, technology, Gen Z, global readiness, diversity, and transparency.

In most states, schools get a rating from the state primarily based on the latest set of education reforms and their accompanying test scores. This is an extremely narrow way to measure 21st century schools. To get a broader picture of school effectiveness, we should be asking:

1. What is the school doing to maintain student safety?

2. How is the school using technology and managing social media?

3. Are the students making progress as measured by test scores, internal formative and summative assessments, or other accountability measures?

4. Has the school taken steps to help the different generations in the teaching staff work together, and has it adapted its teaching and learning space to fit Gen Z?

5. Does the school have a global vision and actively prepare its students to be global ready?

6. How does the school make accepting diversity and maximizing opportunities for all students a critical part of its mission?

7. Is the school considered to be transparent in its intent, operations, and responses?

An old saying about assessment is "What's inspected gets respected!" School leaders already respect these seven disruptions; they should be inspected and used to drive school improvement.

But how do we measure these areas? By thinking about school assessment in a totally different way.

THINKING WITHOUT A BOX

When Tom Friedman interviewed Lin Wells, who teaches at the National Defense University, for his book *Thank You for Being Late*, Wells said there are three ways to solve a problem: "Inside the box . . . outside the box . . . or where there is no box" (T. Friedman). How can this idea be applied to education? In education we spend too much time inside the box, which means we tweak our curriculum and teaching methods to raise test scores or meet other accountability measures. Outside-the-box thinking often just becomes new ways of solving old curriculum and assessment problems.

The world is moving so quickly we can't just sprinkle a few improvements into traditional school evaluation systems and think that will suffice. Instead of living inside or outside the box as educators, we must move to where there is no box, which means we must step far away from our traditional-looking schools and operating procedures and reimagine a system of school goals built around 21st century disruptions and global-readiness initiatives.

We must discard the 20th century lenses. Our educators must be local global leaders; our schools must be local global institutions. And educators, not politicians, must lead the way.

Instead of waiting for the state or federal governments to tell us how to improve, educators need to step into the fray with concrete ideas for improving schools by looking at progress differently. Educators manage a wide range of disruptions on a daily basis; their school assessment system should be broad enough and flexible enough to give them credit for the amazing work they do.

And they need a system that does more than give them a grade or a label; they need a formative system that allows them to focus on the big picture and that helps them thrive in an era of hyper-change.

We shouldn't think this hunt for a better school evaluation is a new process; we've been assessing school progress since *A Nation at Risk* was released 35 years ago. While our schools have adapted significantly since 1983, the world has transformed more quickly than schools (and most private industries) have been able to transform; thus, our nation continues to be at risk if our schools underperform and fail to meet their current challenges. Understanding the disruptions, managing them, and looking to the future will allow American schools to be education leaders in the world—and among all American industries.

A huge goal? Yes. But as we've seen in the previous chapters, a lot of our schools are halfway there in managing a wide range of disruptions. Let's use the still-relevant opening words of *A Nation at Risk* as an excuse to think differently: "Our nation is at risk. Our once unchallenged preeminence in commerce, industry, science, and technological innovation is being overtaken by competitors throughout the world." Let's think of these words as our Educators' Declaration of Independence.

We can't just tweak what we are doing or think a little differently; we need to throw the box away.

A FLEXIBLE, FORMATIVE SCHOOL ASSESSMENT SYSTEM

The disruptions of this century often give school leaders more daily tasks than they can adequately handle. As we propose a new school evaluation system, we can hear their collective voices justifiably saying, "Another new system? Evaluate us more thoroughly?

We have trouble managing the system we have now; how are we supposed to find the time for a huge new system?"

These are valid points. Educators attempting to be freed from a state of future shock should not be burdened with a cumbersome new bureaucratic, test-driven system. They simply don't have time for it. A new all-encompassing school evaluation procedure that is rigidly imposed and done in a threatening manner would drive them deeper into future shock—and some of them would be driven out of the profession.

Instead, the system we are proposing has these qualities:

- It is flexible.

- It is useful.

- It can be implemented in various stages over a period of years.

- It can be implemented differently from school to school. Each school can have its own unique plan.

- It is a dynamic, formative tool for improvement, not a summative assessment of judgment.

- It is a way to measure progress for internal use only, not as a way for external entities to compare schools or give schools new accountability ratings. It should *not* be used in this way.

- It is implemented by schools with their own unique timeline of implementation. Educators are encouraged to think beyond the typical 9-month school year and create a multiyear plan.

- It requires a team effort; schools are dealing with so many disruptions today that progress can't be assessed by administrators alone. To be effective it *must* be done with the help of students, staff, and community members. The days are gone when the superintendents or principals could carry school improvement on their shoulders. There's so much to do, the leadership must be distributed throughout the school.

- Most important, it can be an exciting way for 21st century educators to look closely at areas in which they already have a vested interest and create a way of charting their own progress and steps for improvement. Instead of dealing with an accountability system layered with punitive labels and measures, educators can embrace a system built around what they do on a daily basis.

From this point forward, schools must be flexible and not tied to rigid guidelines. Schools today face the same flexibility challenges as 21st century corporations. Those that pivot quickly will flourish; those stuck in the 20th century will perish.

School leaders can do this if they understand disruptions. Here are nine practical steps for transitioning into a new school evaluation system designed around today's disruptions.

Step 1: Blend Existing Improvement Plans Into the New One

Educators don't have the luxury of abandoning their state-imposed accountability systems to start a new one of their own design. The proposed system to measure disruptions can be used in conjunction with the current school-wide accountability systems designed around education reform initiatives; the new system will simply add the other six global disruptions into the process.

This means educators will have a foot in two systems: the state system from the past and the broader new one of the present and the future. This can be done; American school leaders multitask as well as any leaders in the world. When implemented, an improvement plan designed around the seven disruptions will help educators, and any other parties with whom the educators want to share the plan, to see the progress being made by the school on a broad front and not just in the area of test scores.

In addition, more questions than ever before are being raised about the value of state-mandated tests and their meaning. Are we approaching a day when standardized testing as we know it quickly becomes obsolete? Will technology, especially new forms of artificial intelligence, disrupt education to the point that the reading, writing, and math skills we value today will no longer be needed or tested? Will we be allowed to implement student assessments designed around global readiness and not just multiple-hour tests that measure how well students perform in the core areas? It's time to prepare for the next age of education, one fueled by hyper-change, and a new system of measuring progress that will allow schools to transition more quickly into a remarkably different future. (More on hyper-change will be addressed in Chapter 11.)

Many schools already have some form of improvement plans designed around some of the disruptions; they could easily be folded into one overall plan. For example, some districts have multiyear technology plans that could be used, or they might have school safety plans that have been created with great care and effort. Instead of creating an entirely new plan, these schools could just compile their plans into one and add the new disruption areas they would like to address.

Step 2: Choose How Many Disruptions to Measure

To begin, school leaders should look at the disruptions in their schools; rank their level of importance for their students, staff, and community (refer to the exercise at the end of Chapter 1); and determine how many areas can be addressed in the initial stages of the transition. The number of disruptions measured will vary from school to school. Some might work with three or four areas, and others might cover more.

For example, everyone will have test scores and academic reforms at the top of their list of disruptions to examine. Because of the effort already put into this disruption and due to its political and academic importance, it will be the first disruption placed in the new system.

Every school deals with school safety. That could be the second disruption added to the list. All schools are in various stages of technology implementation; that could be the third element added. Schools could stop there for the first year or keep going. Perhaps more progress is needed in promoting diversity; if so, schools could add that one to study for the year. Or perhaps there have been issues with transparency. Or maybe a unique local disruption has shaken the school; perhaps there has been a rise in alcohol abuse by students, or a parents group is demanding you examine a part of a certain curriculum. These could be worked in as separate disruptions or as part of the ones dealing with student safety or transparency. Each school's plan will be unique based on the hierarchy of concern as determined by the school personnel.

Step 3: Move at the Proper Speed

For many school leaders, expanding quickly from the current system into seven or more disruptions will be overwhelming. This is completely understandable. Leaders and staff should move at a pace that ensures they are making progress; yet they should not do so much that it becomes a perfunctory process or burns out participants. A school might start with three or four disruptions in its first year, and then it might add more as it becomes comfortable with the process. This could be a multiyear process, not one begun in September and ended with the school year in May or June.

Step 4: Ask Four Questions

After choosing the disruptions to measure, leaders should ask their staff, students, and community four simple questions:

1. How are we doing in these seven disruption areas?
2. How do we know?
3. What are our goals moving forward?
4. How will we know we're making progress in meeting our goals this year and beyond?

The preliminary document might look like this:

DISRUPTION AREA	HOW ARE WE DOING IN THIS AREA?	HOW DO WE KNOW?	WHAT ARE OUR GOALS?	HOW DO WE KNOW WE ARE MAKING PROGRESS?
Keeping up with education reforms				
Promoting school safety				
Adapting to new technology				

(Continued)

DISRUPTION AREA	HOW ARE WE DOING IN THIS AREA?	HOW DO WE KNOW?	WHAT ARE OUR GOALS?	HOW DO WE KNOW WE ARE MAKING PROGRESS?
Teaching Gen Z and managing generational differences				
Preparing students to be global ready				
Promoting diversity				
Maintaining transparency in operations				

Step 5: Implement the CAT Process in the New Improvement Plan

To successfully deal with disruptions, to learn from them, and to use them to their advantage, school leaders must work with their staff to

- cope with disruptive events in the first 24 to 48 hours of the event to ascertain what has happened,

- adjust policies and procedures in the weeks following the event to prevent the next event or be better prepared to deal with it, and

- transform their thinking and philosophies in the months after the event so they and their staff can continue to grow and move forward as 21st century thinkers.

This can be a reflective component to the plan. To integrate the CAT process, school leaders could add a CAT column for each disruption area and ask, "Was CAT used this year in each area? If so, for how many events? How did the school transform its culture and practices?"

Step 6: Use Qualitative and Quantitative Data to Help Determine Progress

There are two ways to measure progress in managing disruptions: by using quantitative data and by using qualitative data. If hard numbers are available to gauge progress, then they can be used; but many of these areas will also need anecdotal evidence or measurements not deriving from traditional sources, especially as schools begin the process.

Some of the quantitative measures will require new ways of collecting data, but it doesn't have to be costly or time-consuming; it could often require a commitment to keeping track of what is already occurring. And many of the qualitative measures could be turned into quantitative measures if a school decides to implement a survey to augment anecdotal responses.

Here are some examples.

DISRUPTION AREA TO BE MEASURED	EXAMPLE OF QUANTITATIVE DATA	EXAMPLE OF QUALITATIVE DATA
Keeping up with education reforms	What are the test data and other data compiled for the traditional evaluation system?	Do students, parents, and educators agree or disagree with the current system?
Promoting school safety	How many violent incidents occurred this year?	Are we hearing of more stress in our student body?
Adapting to new technology	How many laptops, tablets, or other devices were implemented this year?	What are the trends we're seeing among our students with apps and device uses?
Teaching Gen Z and managing generational differences	How many hours of professional development did we devote to studying ways to teach Gen Z?	What are our students telling us about their dreams and fears?
Preparing students to be global ready	How many times this year did our teachers implement the 4Cs in their curriculum?	Did we find ways for students who have traveled abroad or moved here from another country to discuss their travels?

(Continued)

(Continued)

DISRUPTION AREA TO BE MEASURED	EXAMPLE OF QUANTITATIVE DATA	EXAMPLE OF QUALITATIVE DATA
Promoting diversity	How many plans do we have in place to promote diversity?	What are the greatest challenges we have with regard to diversity?
Maintaining transparency	How many complaints did we get this year from students, parents, or community members who said they didn't know enough about school operations or funding?	Is our website adequate, or should we spend more time and money on it to make it more robust?

Step 7: Ask Questions for Each Disruption Area

Groups of educators, students, parents, and community members who are working with school leaders to implement a new accountability system should form questions about the chosen disruptions and measuring progress. Here are some ideas for each area, with three questions to start the conversations. More questions could be added by each school based on its concerns.

Keeping Up With Education Reforms

Schools have ample data about their work in this disruption area. It could be centered on test scores, graduation rates, attendance rates, college readiness, value added, or myriad other measurements. This is the disruption area in which we've lived for the past three decades; it's gotten the most attention and will continue to do so as long as it is the sole determiner of measuring our success by state and national officials. As school leaders create a new, broader evaluation system, managing this disruption will be a continuation of prior efforts. While schools need to take a broader look at how they gauge their progress, testing and other accountability measures should not be ignored. They measure student progress in key areas, and the consequences from the states are often serious. Plus, this is the disruption area the parents and general public are most used to seeing; it's still a vital part of our operations and planning.

Here are three questions to begin the conversation about evaluating education reforms:

1. How do we improve student success in our state accountability domains?

2. Are there academic concerns beyond the state accountability system?

3. How do we balance this disruption area with others in our new accountability system?

Promoting Student Safety

Most schools have school safety plans designed to help ensure student and staff safety. But *school safety* is a broad term. This area could also include school violence, alcohol and drug abuse, dating violence, eating disorders, mental health concerns, and all the efforts already in place to address them and other student safety issues. Of course, the idea is to step back and take a broad look at what is happening and to systemize the efforts to address the problems. Placing school safety beside the student test scores in a new evaluation system would be a great way to show the community that safety is valued and programs are in place to help young people.

Here are three questions to begin the conversation about evaluating school safety:

1. Do we have a broad school safety plan in place?

2. What are our biggest concerns with regard to student safety?

3. What initiatives do we have in place around school safety and student wellness, and which ones should we add?

Adapting to New Technology

Technology implementation at the district level and in the classroom will transform education in the next two decades; it's imperative that school leaders have a system in place for implementing technology, maintaining it, training educators in its use, and just as important, looking to the future to see the software programs and devices that are coming so they can be quickly assimilated into instruction. Technology is speeding up; schools must keep pace with their thinking, vision, and implementation.

Here are three questions to start the conversation about evaluating technology efforts:

1. Do we have a broad technology plan in place?

2. What technology are we using at the district and classroom level, and which parts of it are effective and ineffective?

3. What practices do we have in place to ensure digital citizenship is embedded in our school culture?

Teaching Gen Z and Managing Generational Differences

Today's students are different, and future generations will continue to evolve with technology and shifts in lifestyles. Educators need to adjust their teaching styles, expectations, and skills to serve today's students, and they must continue to adapt for the rest of their careers to the needs of the next generation.

Here are three questions to start the conversation about evaluating efforts to teach Gen Z and manage generational differences in a staff:

1. Have we studied Gen Z to become aware of its learning styles?

2. Have we discussed different philosophies among different generations in the teaching staff?

3. How can we include some of our Gen Z students in our planning as we move forward?

Preparing Students to Be Global Ready

Our task is complex: to prepare students to be successful in a connected world that is rapidly evolving. Technology will continue to alter lifestyles, the business community is becoming flatter, and Gen Z students are exposed to more world issues through the Internet and social media than any generation before them. A number of today's infants, because of the health advances that will be brought about by supercomputers, might live for 150 years. How do we prepare them for this world?

Here are three questions to start the conversation about evaluating efforts to help students be global ready:

1. What does it mean for a student to be global ready?

2. How do we balance the state-imposed curriculum and testing with the need to stress global skills?

3. How are we connecting students and staff with exterior experts in today's high-tech, connected world?

Promoting Diversity

American society and our schools are growing more diverse. Part of the charter of all schools is to be accepting places where all kinds of students are welcomed and educated; however, there are constant new challenges encountered as school leaders deal with shifting populations, ethnic and cultural differences, and gender questions. School leaders now deal with issues they never imagined 30 years ago, and they will encounter new challenges in the future.

Here are three questions to start the conversation about evaluating diversity initiatives:

1. Do our students and staff consider our school to be an accepting and nurturing environment for all kinds of individuals?

2. What issues have we encountered in the past year?

3. What programs do we have in place to promote diversity and to help students assimilate academically while maintaining their individuality?

Maintaining Transparency in Operations

Parents and community members want to be more informed than ever about what is happening in schools, and public schools are under increasingly tight scrutiny regarding how they operate and spend money. The advent of social media, online grade-reporting systems, and open records requests has added a new set of expectations to the role of school leaders: They must be prepared to document for the public what they did and why they did it.

Here are three questions to start the conversation about evaluating transparency in operations:

1. What are we currently doing to be transparent with students, parents, and the community in how we operate?

2. Have we had any transparency issues within the past year?

3. What can we do in the future to proactively remain transparent without allowing it to become a costly burden that consumes too much energy, money, and time?

Step 8: Score the Disruption Initiatives for Internal Purposes (Optional)

Some educators might prefer to create a scoring or labeling system for the plan so they can chart progress. This is an optional step. A committee working on the project would establish benchmarks in each area and devise a simple scoring system, perhaps holistically, for progress made in achieving the benchmarks. The overall score could add up to 100% or any other desired number. Or to avoid numerical grades, schools could use terminology such as *incomplete, in progress,* or *successful.*

Remember, a school might not want to start by working in *all* the areas in its first year of implementation. Each school should make the shift at its own pace and develop its own assessment system. And another reminder: This is meant to be a formative tool used internally, not a rigid instrument dissected in the local press and thrust on schools by exterior parties. Schools might choose *never* to score their initiative and choose to use the chart in their own way to move into the future. The scoring should only be done if the schools are confident in their educational and political status.

Step 9: Start by Shifting Mindsets—and Never Stop Shifting

While administrators might have a vision of how the new assessment plan could work, their students, staff, and communities will not. If the administrator suddenly calls a meeting and announces the intention of implementing the new plan without first laying the foundation for profound change, then the plan will suffer the fate of many other well-intentioned school initiatives: It will be an abject failure that disillusions stakeholders and makes the next iteration even harder to implement.

Here are four things school leaders can do to lay the foundation for shifting mindsets and implementing a new school-wide appraisal system.

1. *Help stakeholders understand the need to transform.*

   American school leaders and stakeholders must have a common vision.

   - They must acknowledge that they work in an education world filled with disruptions.
   - They need to understand the origins of the disruptions.
   - They need to understand the waves of American school history and how they tie into today's turbulent education environment.
   - They must be forward-thinking to anticipate future disruptions, including disruptions that don't yet exist.
   - They must share the vision with others to bring them along on the journey; it can't be done without a team.

2. *Distribute leadership throughout the school and the implementation process.*

   Moving schools today is too big of a project for school leaders to attempt alone; they need the assistance and input of teachers, parents, community members, and students. Schools today often have school improvement teams in place. Perhaps the goals for these teams could be realigned, or the team could be expanded to incorporate the new plan for dealing with disruptions.

3. *Dedicate 25% of professional development activities to thinking without the box.*

   Thinking inside the box will improve the current system in a traditional way; thinking outside the box will improve the current system in a nontraditional way; thinking without the box encourages people to create a new system. We live in an accelerated era. There will be times when we must step beyond the normal thinking to create a new system or at least a new part of it. Build this part of your professional development around questions such as these:

   - *Instead of thinking about what must be done, think "What if we could . . . ?"*
   - *What we think of as magical now will be occurring in our classrooms within the next 10 to 20 years. What will that look like and how will we use it?*

4. *Create a timeline of implementation . . . and then throw away the calendar.*

All improvement plans need a timeline with steps and benchmarks, including this new version of measuring school improvement—but a difference is that this one never ends. School leaders usually implement 9-month plans that can be implemented and assessed during a school year, and then they start over the next year with new goals. This one needs a calendar for initial implementation, but there's no end date. We're not going to see an end to disruptions; some disruptions might rise or fall in importance as the world shifts, and new disruptions will be added as the world changes, but this format and mindset of coping, adjusting, and transforming will continue for the rest of our careers.

AN EXAMPLE OF A NEW ASSESSMENT INSTRUMENT

Here's a basic outline of a new, internal assessment instrument built around 21st century disruptions that can be used after the planning has been made and work is in progress. This tool can be used throughout the school year or at the end of a school year to measure success, to refocus efforts, and to plan for the future. Each plan can be unique to the school with different areas, indicators, and scoring systems (or non-scoring systems). The complexity of the tool will vary depending on the needs and desires of the school.

AREAS OF FOCUS AND INDICATORS OF SUCCESS	HOW DO WE KNOW?	WHAT SCORE SHOULD WE GIVE OUR EFFORTS AND RESULTS?	WHAT ARE OUR PLANS FOR MOVING FORWARD?
KEEPING UP WITH EDUCATION REFORMS			
• Did we improve student success in our state accountability domains?			
• Did we address academic concerns beyond the state accountability system?			

AREAS OF FOCUS AND INDICATORS OF SUCCESS	HOW DO WE KNOW?	WHAT SCORE SHOULD WE GIVE OUR EFFORTS AND RESULTS?	WHAT ARE OUR PLANS FOR MOVING FORWARD?
• Did we balance this disruption area with others in our new accountability system?			
PROMOTING STUDENT SAFETY			
• Was our school safety plan effectively implemented this year?			
• What issues were effectively handled?			
• How did we improve the school safety plan this year?			
ADAPTING TO NEW TECHNOLOGY			
• Did we have a broad technology plan in place?			
• What technology was effective and ineffective?			
• Did we embed digital citizenship into the school culture?			
TEACHING GEN Z AND MANAGING GENERATIONAL DIFFERENCES			
• Did we study Gen Z to become aware of its learning styles?			
• Did we study generational differences within the teaching staff?			

(Continued)

(Continued)

AREAS OF FOCUS AND INDICATORS OF SUCCESS	HOW DO WE KNOW?	WHAT SCORE SHOULD WE GIVE OUR EFFORTS AND RESULTS?	WHAT ARE OUR PLANS FOR MOVING FORWARD?
• Did we include some of our Gen Z students in our planning?			
PREPARING STUDENTS TO BE GLOBAL READY			
• Did we define what it means for a student to be global ready?			
• How did we balance the state-imposed curriculum with the need to teach global skills?			
• How did we connect students and staff to exterior experts?			
PROMOTING DIVERSITY			
• Do our students and staff consider our school to be an accepting and nurturing environment for all kinds of individuals?			
• What issues did we encounter in the past year?			
• What programs do we have in place to promote diversity and to help students assimilate academically while maintaining their individuality?			

AREAS OF FOCUS AND INDICATORS OF SUCCESS	HOW DO WE KNOW?	WHAT SCORE SHOULD WE GIVE OUR EFFORTS AND RESULTS?	WHAT ARE OUR PLANS FOR MOVING FORWARD?
MAINTAINING TRANSPARENCY IN OPERATIONS			
• Were we transparent with students, parents, and the community in our operations?			
• Were there any transparency issues this year?			
• Did we remain transparent while balancing energy, money, and time?			

Our progress should be measured in the most important areas to affect our schools today with the understanding that our schools will be disrupted in the future. They must morph into new types of organizations. We need maximum flexibility and efficiency—because the fifth wave of American school history is about to wash over us: the Hyper-Change Age.

CREATE YOUR OWN PLAN FOR LEADING IN DISRUPTIVE TIMES

1. Form a group of teachers, parents, community members, and students (if age appropriate) to help you form a new evaluation plan for your school.

2. Share the vision with the group.

3. Review the disruptions you listed at the end of Chapter 2 and share the list with the group.

4. Decide on how many disruptions you want to address in the first steps.

5. Have the group rank the disruptions in order of importance for your school. Give priority to the disruptions that are most important.

6. Discuss each disruption and begin to ask:
   - How are we doing in this area?
   - How do we know?
   - What are our goals?
   - How do we know we're making progress?

7. Break out each disruption area into measurable benchmarks. There might be some areas in which you don't have hard data. For example, you might decide you need a new program to assist students with mental health issues in the disruption area of school safety. Measuring that could mean you and the group have examined programs, you have implemented one, and students are being serviced. You can always go back in the next iteration and add data about how many students are being serviced and what they are telling you about the program. Keep the initial steps simple. You can add the benchmarks to this chart or create a separate one of your own design.

8. Fill in the chart on page 201 to begin your efforts.

9. Create a timeline by adding another column to this chart or create a separate one of your own design.

10. Convert the planning chart mentioned above into an assessment tool by creating benchmarks beside the bullets as shown on page 202–203. Remember, you might not want to address all the disruptions above in your initial plan, and you can add your own local disruptions to the plan to make it more viable. Add your own areas of measurement across the top of the tool and your own indicators of success for each disruption, and score it (or don't score it) as you see necessary, or use the ones listed above. The essential question is: **How do we know we are looking beyond test scores to meet the needs of 21st century students who need to be global ready in a rapidly shifting society and economy?**

DISRUPTION AREA	HOW ARE WE DOING IN THIS AREA?	HOW DO WE KNOW?	WHAT ARE OUR GOALS?	HOW DO WE KNOW WE ARE MAKING PROGRESS?	WHAT SCORE WOULD WE GIVE TO OUR PROGRESS IN THIS AREA?
Keeping up with education reforms					
Promoting school safety					
Adapting to new technology					
Teaching Gen Z and managing generational differences					
Preparing students to be global ready					
Promoting diversity					
Maintaining transparency in operations					
Local Disruption 1					
Local Disruption 2					

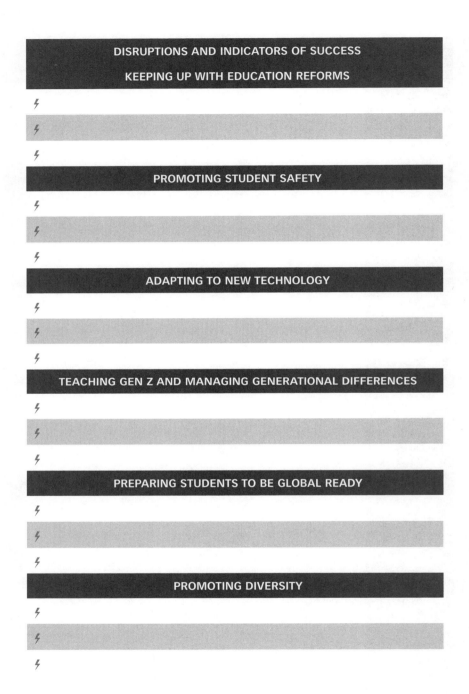

DISRUPTIONS AND INDICATORS OF SUCCESS

KEEPING UP WITH EDUCATION REFORMS

PROMOTING STUDENT SAFETY

ADAPTING TO NEW TECHNOLOGY

TEACHING GEN Z AND MANAGING GENERATIONAL DIFFERENCES

PREPARING STUDENTS TO BE GLOBAL READY

PROMOTING DIVERSITY

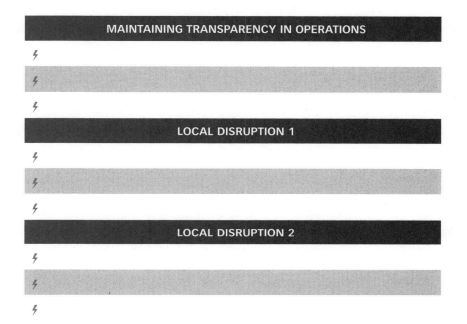

MAINTAINING TRANSPARENCY IN OPERATIONS

LOCAL DISRUPTION 1

LOCAL DISRUPTION 2

An Accelerating World

Leading Schools in an Age of Hyper-Change

We are living in a new period of hyper-change. The speed at which our world is changing is unprecedented, and that transformation is the central reality of our lives. The technology revolution is now carrying us with it at a speed beyond our imagining toward ever newer technologically shaped realities that often appear, in the words of Arthur C. Clarke, "indistinguishable from magic."

—Al Gore, *The Future* (Freeland)

Have schools entered an era of hyper-change?

Hyper-change can be described as a period when changes arrive in quickening succession and stack on the previous changes with deepening impact. In other words, the iterations speed up, become more complex, and leave us perplexed and racing to understand what is happening. This sequence can be found when studying American education reforms in the past three decades:

- 1983: *A Nation at Risk*
- 2001: No Child Left Behind

- 2010: Race to the Top and the Common Core
- 2015: Every Student Succeeds Act

Now notice the pace of the implementation:

- From 1983 to 2001 is 18 years.
- From 2001 to 2010 is 9 years.
- From 2010 to 2015 is 5 years.

Not only are our national reform movements accelerating, but the period between each initiative has been *cut in half*. Each one was built on the previous change, and the impact of each initiative was deeper than that of the previous initiative. As American politicians, educators, and community members grappled with global accelerations, they churned out massive improvement efforts at ever-faster rates, culminating in the dizzying array of standards and tests that now dominate American education.

When we examine the results of these acts, their pacing, and the other disruptions rocking American schools, a case can be made that American educators (who are already groping their way out of a future shock) are about to enter an era of hyper-change—or have already entered it.

It will bring *profound changes* to American education.

While we might consider the changes of the past three decades to be tumultuous, there are signs that those disruptions will be minor in comparison with the changes school leaders will encounter in the next three decades. Think of the disruptions since 1983 as the squall lines of an approaching hurricane. They have come ashore in quicker succession, and we have noticed their rain and gale-force winds. But the big storm, the hurricane of hyper-change, is still offshore; it's a Category 5 monster coming at us. When it reaches shore its impact will be massive, and education as we know it will be altered forever.

But here's an essential point for today's educators: While real hurricanes are massively *destructive*, this approaching storm can be radically *constructive*. If we greet it with the proper mindset and employ its amazing technology effectively, we can create classrooms in which magic is a daily occurrence.

A GLIMPSE OF SCHOOL FUTURES: DIGITIZATION, DISRUPTION, AND DEMOCRATIZATION

When author Tom Friedman interviewed Tom Wujec, a global leader in 3-D design, engineering, and entertainment software, and asked him about future change, Wujec said all "industries are becoming computable. When an industry becomes computable, it goes through a series of predictable changes. It moves from being digitized to being disrupted to being democratized" (T. Friedman).

What does this mean for schools? We've gone from the 3Rs of the 20th century to the 4Cs of the 21st century—and now we are moving into the 3Ds of hyper-change. First schools will be digitized. Then they will be disrupted. Then they will be democratized.

To get a clue of what will happen to schools, let's define these three terms.

- *Digitized*: When most of the school functions, including the majority of teaching and learning, are based on the latest technology that will include a deepening cloud, new types of devices, and increasingly robust artificial intelligence.

- *Disrupted*: When the technology dramatically changes how teachers instruct and how students learn. Learning will take place where students have access to technology, not just in schools.

- *Democratization*: When students have a much greater choice in how they learn, where they learn, what they learn, the pace at which they learn, and how they are assessed.

To get a better idea of what will happen to schools, let's look at how the 3Ds have already reshaped other fields:

- **Clothing:** Instead of buying clothes in a store, people can order online or even design their own clothing.

- **Transportation:** Instead of taking a cab, people can use an app to summon Uber or Lyft.

- **The hotel industry:** Instead of staying in a hotel, people can rent a room or apartment at the Airbnb website.

- **Publishing:** People can buy a book in a bookstore, or they can buy it online at Amazon and have it shipped to them or download it to a device.

- **Graphic design:** People can go to a printer, or they can go online and design their own stationery, business cards, or signs.

- **Travel:** People can book their own airfare, housing, and rental cars, or they can go online and purchase entire trips through Travelocity or Expedia (with discounts).

- **Music composition:** People can purchase music, or they can download music software and compose their own pieces that will be played back on their computers or iPods.

Each of these fields used to be dominated by experts. Now technology allows people to have a much wider choice in how they receive a product and, in many cases, design the product. In each field, the established hierarchy was quickly disrupted and the leaders had to adjust—or be put out of business. Not long ago huge companies in these areas were unchallenged; now they are fighting to remain relevant in *an era when people want more choices in everything they do.*

Could the same thing happen in education because of rapid advances in technology? Could it disrupt our schools even more dramatically than what we are seeing today? Could this lead to a democratization in education when students demand and are granted much more freedom in choosing their learning paths?

Yes.

Let's look more closely at what the 3Ds will do to education.

DIGITIZATION IN EDUCATION

Education is already being digitized. We have more devices than ever before in our schools. When computers first arrived in schools in the form of shared computer labs and a few stand-alone computers, we couldn't have comprehended a day when they would be prevalent in schools to the point that teachers would be putting assignments and assessments online for use in school and at home. Nor could we have envisioned information management systems that allow students and parents to have instant access to information. And we've added distance learning, online learning, and flipped learning. More options are becoming available for students and parents.

More choices will keep coming. One visionary principal, Carrie Jackson of Timberview Middle School in Fort Worth, Texas, sees technology playing an even bigger role in classrooms of the future.

Stories From Exceptional Educational Leaders

Carrie Jackson, Principal
Timberview Middle School
Fort Worth, Texas

I think it (technology) will continue to be streamlined and become more easily accessible. Lots of students and staff have devices on watches now. I see the device access continuing to get smaller/leaner and more purposeful. Already we have digital device access as common as accessing a pencil or pen. For some of us, we reach for the device BEFORE we reach for the pencil or pen. In the near future I just see it becoming more and more commonplace, with some fun tweaks to what the devices can do and access.

I think we are at a place where we need to stop looking at technology as a "thing" and just assume its presence and utility, just as we would any other resource. It's there; we know it's there. Let's just put it to work to make learning even easier, more real, and more fun for kids. Digital leadership? Nope, it's just leadership. Digital is just a part of life . . . and as with any other resource, when leveraged for good it's an awesome help to us.

Jackson makes an essential point: Technology isn't a "thing" anymore; now it's a regular part of 21st century life. Its impact will continue to grow. This is just the beginning of the digitization.

School leaders must also be aware of the revolutionary devices and practices that are just beyond the horizon; they are on the way.

Here are four technology advances that will transform the school landscape within the next decade. School leaders should be among the first to recognize their importance and to implement them in school classrooms and staff training.

1. Virtual Reality

Virtual reality (VR) is already used in a number of schools around the world. An article by Elizabeth Reede and Larissa Bailiff on the site *TechCrunch* in January 2016 detailed the impact VR will have on schools as they become more digitized.

> *Many classes have used VR tools to collaboratively construct architectural models, recreations of historic or natural sites and other spatial renderings. Instructors also have used VR technology to engage students in topics related to literature, history and economics by offering a deeply immersive sense of place and time, whether historic or evolving.*
>
> *. . . VR content and access will undoubtedly influence a pedagogical shift as these new technologies allow a literature teacher in Chicago to "take" her students to Verona to look at the setting for Shakespeare's* Romeo and Juliet, *or a teacher in the Bronx to "bring" her Ancient Civilizations class to the ancient Mayan ruins at Chichen Itza.* (Reede and Bailiff)

Reede and Bailiff point to a steady growth of interest in VR and the companies dedicated to bringing it into schools with "packaged educational curriculum and content, teacher training and the technological tools to support VR-based instruction in the classroom." It's already being used in the United States and Europe, and VR is like other technology: When it is produced on an increasingly greater scale, the price goes down. Reede and Bailiff point out that the investment in VR is expected to hit *$200 billion* by the year 2020; it will rapidly become more abundant and affordable in education.

Imagine the impact on teaching. One of the greatest compliments teachers ever get is when students say the teaching made learning "come alive." With VR, the student will strap on some goggles and fly across the Grand Canyon, tour the Louvre, dive *The Titanic*, explore the chambers of the human heart, navigate the inside of volcanoes, and examine the arches of the Roman Colosseum.

Instead of waiting for a great teacher to describe something, VR will allow the student to step into it or fly around it.

2. The Deepening Cloud

The cloud is not yet fully developed. While we might see new devices today, a hidden fact is that the devices are running off cloud-based technologies that are being constantly improved.

While we already have a number of programs in the cloud, its deepening will allow it to be accessible in more places and to host a greater number of activities.

More textbooks can go online with constant updates; real-time changes are critical because as the world accelerates, textbooks will grow obsolete more quickly. Cloud-based applications will allow schools to purchase cheaper devices, and software will be bought with subscriptions instead of the more expensive seat licenses (Bhatia).

And a stronger cloud will lead to a spread of increasingly complex artificial intelligence (AI). This is where digitization will shake current education practices to their foundations. Think of the cloud as the hidden fog of progress; it's everywhere, it's complex, it's growing thicker, and it will be essential for education to keep expanding.

Put another way, the cloud is just beginning to reshape our classrooms. We can only dream of where it will take us.

3. Artificial Intelligence

How important will AI be in education? Pearson, one of the world's largest makers of traditional assessments, has already studied AI and is preparing for a day in the near future when AI dominates education. Pearson released a study in 2016 titled *Intelligence Unleashed: An Argument for AI in Education* (which Pearson refers to in this excerpt as AIEd).

First, AIEd has the tools and techniques to conduct the fine-grained analysis that allows us to track each learner's development of skills and capabilities as they interact and learn over time. This tracking of individual learners can then be collated and interpreted as required to provide knowledge about progress at the school, district, and country level. . . . The increasing range of data capture devices—such as biological data, voice recognition, and eye tracking—will enable AIEd systems to provide new types of evidence for currently difficult to assess skills. (Luckin et al.)

Biological data? Voice recognition? Eye tracking? It sounds like science fiction, but the technology is coming to classrooms. Biological data will allow schools, and testing companies, to understand more about the correlation between maturity, body growth, brain development, and learning. Voice recognition will allow students to speak into the computer instead of typing, and eye tracking will allow teachers to track a student's eye as it scans a computer screen. Software will then match the eye movement with content and assessment to see how much time was spent on the topic and how to create screen content that appeals to the learner.

This technology might be used in schools, but imagine the ethical questions it will raise as teachers and administrators collect real-time data on what their students are doing in their homes at night. Will it be accepted as progress, or will it be considered too intrusive and be compared to being watched by Big Brother (Orwell)?

It will be possible for AI to collect massive amounts of information, synthesize it, and provide immediate feedback that can be used to adjust the content to better meet the needs of the individual learner, which could make teaching and learning much more efficient.

AI will allow struggling students, especially those in less developed parts of the world, to have access to high-quality, differentiated instruction at an affordable price from an early age. Suddenly, the education gap that has always existed between affluent and impoverished countries could be greatly diminished. Think of the possibilities if the world begins to find well-developed learners in every part of the globe. How many great minds will the world gain that would have previously been lost to poverty? Think of what can happen in future generations when an increase in the well-educated people around the globe can team with AI to attempt to solve more of the world's problems.

Ultimately, AI will be the major force that disrupts teaching. The role of teachers will shift from disseminating content and assessing learning to aligning the content and helping the student with technology applications. Note that the study cites the importance of using AI "alongside the expertise and empathy that is peculiarly human." Teachers will still be needed to bring humanity into the lives of young people—but in the absence of humans AI will suffice.

Put another way, in the hurricane of hyper-change, the deepening cloud is the eye wall, which is the strongest part at the center of the storm, and AI is the eye of the hurricane, the core of the storm. It's getting closer each day. School leaders need to recognize the signs and begin to help their teachers imagine how to use it.

4. Holograms

When we think of holograms, we often think of *Star Wars.* Remember Luke Skywalker standing next to R2-D2 and watching a hologram of Princess Lea pleading for help? Or the Michael Jackson hologram dancing onstage with live performers at the 2014 Billboard Music Awards? These types of holograms are coming to a classroom near you. It's just a matter of time before the details are resolved and they become commonplace in classrooms—which means they'll pop up on the floor, in the middle of the room, in corners, on students' desks, on the teacher's desk, in the halls, or anyplace else in school or out of school where learning is taking place with technology.

Some educators are already thinking of how they will be used in education. A recent article from the International Society for Technology in Education (ISTE) lists eight ways holograms will affect learning:

1. *Students will work with other students, teachers or experts worldwide in what feels like face-to-face interaction. . . .*

2. *Holograms could allow students to conduct science experiments that would be too dangerous, too expensive or too difficult to perform in real life.*

3. *Students could tour historical sites in 3D and have their questions answered by a hologram. . . .*

4. *Gaming would become truly immersive and would allow students to interact with the environments they create.*

5. *Students in classrooms or makerspaces could complete a design project in three dimensions. . . .*

6. *Instructors could deliver lessons and lectures to multiple classrooms, across the globe, simultaneously.*

7. *After testing for motor skill development using holographic technology, scientists could analyze the data to create software to improve motor skills for students with muscular or coordination difficulties.*

8. *Holograms could train students how to do job-related tasks in vocational fields of interest.* (ISTE Connects)

Students will interact with holograms of their teachers, other teachers, professors, and experts, throughout the school, at home, or in other parts of the world. Instead of watching a video of the Battle of Waterloo, students will see a reenactment on the floor of their classroom. Instead of seeing a picture of Martin Luther King Jr. marching in Selma, AI and holograms will allow students to interview him as he sits in a desk beside them. Instead of seeing pictures of exhibits in the New York Museum of Art, students will find those exhibits in the classroom. Instead of the entire class working out with a PE teacher, some students will go to another part of the gym to be led by a hologram of an Olympic athlete.

And that's just the beginning.

HOW EDUCATION WILL BE DISRUPTED

Today, if a teacher is a technology leader, it means the teacher effectively incorporates tablets, laptops, and other existing technology in the classroom; it is considered to be a "technology-rich" environment. We now can see that much deeper levels of technology are coming—which means this is just the first iteration of education technology; we are in the infant stages. Within a decade we will look back at our current software and tablets in the same way we now look back at VCRs, camcorders, car phones, and Atari video games as relics from the time when technology first was entering our lives.

In the future, technology leaders will be incorporating more VR, more blended learning and flipped learning using holograms, stronger software in the cloud, and more AI to tie it together and tailor instruction for every individual student.

In other words, being technology literate as an educator in the future will be much different from what it is today. Today we use technology to augment education; in the future it will be the base for the vast majority of what is done in education.

And that's just for the future we can see from today's vantage point. By the time we get there, newer types of technology will be approaching on the horizon, types we have not yet imagined.

When students have access to AI, they will no longer have to wait for a teacher to control all aspects of their learning. Depending on the age of the student and the philosophy/availability of the parents, students might do some of their work in school, but they could also spend more time at home doing exploratory learning projects, internships, and other activities during time normally spent in school. Because they will have access to so much more of what they need to be educated, they will have much more control of their learning. They will no longer be just the recipients; they will become partners and co-owners.

But here is the most important point for teachers to know: Their days of being the primary disseminators of information are numbered. They will have to rapidly pivot to become facilitators of information gathering. Those teachers who find themselves in this transition period in the early or middle part of their careers will have to adjust or find themselves irrelevant. Teachers who insist on controlling the content, delivery of instruction, pacing, and assessment will become obsolete and will not have a place in 21st century schools.

The role of school leadership will also be transformed. Administrators will need to help teachers access the latest technology and programs, help them constantly transition from one technology advance to the next, and work with students, teachers, and parents to help students measure their learning, which means instead of implementing broad new school-wide initiatives, administrators will be working with teachers to adjust the instruction and assessment of individual students or small groups of students. Will the school leadership models we espouse today still be useful then?

In the near future, understanding how to use technology will be the most essential skill to be learned. The traditional curriculum designed around students' learning key elements of literature, mathematics, science, and social studies will be obsolete. They will still need to use those disciplines, but technology will be the tool they use to navigate through them. Education futurist Marc Prensky has written:

> *In these digital times, is it still worthwhile to teach students how to write by hand, calculate in their heads, read, and define words and concepts—that is, most of the elementary school curriculum? Or is that like teaching kids how to hunt for their food? That was useful—once. . . . Suppose we were to rethink our curriculum . . . without any preconceived notions of what was important, caring only about students' future needs.*

Think of what Prensky is saying when he compares the usefulness of some of our curriculum with "teaching kids how to hunt for their food." Much of our curriculum is about to be rendered obsolete when it is overtaken by advances in technology.

To rethink our goals, Prensky says we should focus on four critical areas:

> *Effective Thinking, which would include creative and critical thinking as well as portions of math, science, logic, persuasion, and even storytelling; Effective Action, which would include entrepreneurship, goal setting, planning, persistence, project management, and feedback; and Effective Relationships, which would include emotional intelligence, teamwork, ethics, and more.*

> *The remainder of this curriculum would focus on Effective Accomplishment—what you do with what you've learned. That part would be entirely project-based and real-world oriented and would differ for every student.*

And if we could do this, then standardized test scores—those 20th century benchmarks that have been carried into the 21st century—could finally be cast aside.

Some critics who complain schools aren't transforming quickly enough say that they are museums of the past; their square class-rooms and straight rows of student desks are a better fit for the world of 30 years ago than for the globalization of today. As education becomes democratized, schools truly could become museums—empty ones students will visit to see how young people used to be educated with bells, mass feedings in cafeterias, stan-dardized tests, and much more rigid pathways to learning.

Perhaps we are in the final wave of brick-and-mortar schooling. Technology will allow schools of the future to be democratized; they will be smaller, decentralized, and more personalized. The rush of technology could occur so quickly that some school build-ings, especially high schools that are recently built and meant to be financed over a 30- to 40-year period, could be half empty before they are paid off. Today we talk about methods of incorporating new types of furniture into schools to keep up with the learning styles of Gen Z. This could be the last evolution in school furniture and design—because many of the students won't be there in the future.

They'll be learning in new types of schools or anywhere they can tap into technology.

HOW EDUCATION WILL BE DEMOCRATIZED

What has happened in other industries will happen in education. Our field will be dramatically digitized, disrupted on a scale we can barely imagine, and then education democratization will emerge from our 20th century models. As technology advances, prices will come down and education will leap beyond traditional school buildings, school days, school years, school teachers, and school administrators.

- Democratization will allow learning to occur in more places. Education will no longer have to be found exclusively in schools; depending on the age of the student, it can be any-where there are devices, the cloud, AI, and holograms. It might be in a school, or it might be in some type of small learning center at the end of the street—or in a bedroom or basement.

- Democratization will allow more students to be working at their own pace on their own development track. The ramifications for a more personalized learning system built around learning styles, interests, and global skills that don't require standardized core testing as we know it will change how we view a student's education progress. This could eliminate the needs of present-day gifted programs or special education programs. And when students of all ability levels successfully go deeper into their learning with more relevancy and rigor, their overall education improves.

- Education will no longer be the sole domain of educators; people with limited expertise in leading schools will be able to effectively open new types of learning centers if they have access to the devices and software.

This democratization will create a flurry of questions for school leaders. In the future, administrators will have to lead the way in answering:

- What will be the role of teachers, curriculum, and administrators when students can interact with AI, holograms, and VR?

- How has this shift from a formal structure to more of an independent system affected students emotionally?

- How much time should be provided in school or some other setting for students to socialize and develop their interaction skills?

- What new ethical issues will students encounter as they become more dependent on stronger and wider-reaching technology? For example, as AI becomes more advanced do we need to carefully pace student exposure to certain topics to ensure it is age appropriate? As students begin to interact with historical holograms, should we carefully monitor the software to ensure it will provide an appropriate learning experience? The ethical quandaries will be significant.

- The arts in schools fill a vital creative void for students; what will be their place and that of other electives in a disrupted education environment?

- How should schools continue to transform their classrooms to make use of more technology and the learning skills of this generation and future generations who will be growing up with deeper technology skills and new expectations?

Society will need experts to guide its young people. Teachers will still be needed to nurture students, monitor the technology, and fill in the gaps in learning. School leaders will be needed to lead the programming and, most important, show people the power of the new education system.

In other words, within the next 15 years, administrators will be closing out a 20th century education model at the same time they are pulling stakeholders into a 21st century technology-laden system with new types of students in a new type of world with new types of schools.

Did we mention these are tough jobs?

OVERCOMING THREE BARRIERS

Hyper-change in education could be the finest development in education history if we embrace it and move quickly to adjust with it.

Of course, education will undergo massive variations from what we know today. The question is not whether the technology is coming or whether a new system of education is arriving in the future; the question is, will educators survive the professional transition and accept the new realities?

Barriers That Could Hold School Leaders Back From Embracing Hyper-Change

1. An inability to break out of the current mold because of philosophical/political resistance

2. The turnover rate of school leaders

3. An inability to change the current job structure of overburdened teachers and administrators

---

Will we have the courage to embrace the disruptions, or will we hold fast to the past? Will the different powerful forces guiding education have the flexibility and vision to transform, or will greed and a lack of vision hold them back?

Let's take a closer look at the barriers to understand them.

Barrier 1: Preserving the Status Quo

On January 17, 1961, while American schools were being shaped by the Nuclear Age, President Dwight Eisenhower warned the nation about the power of the emerging "military-industrial complex." In Ike's words, the nation was threatened by the growing influence of the American military and American industry ("Eisenhower Warns of Military-Industrial Complex").

Today we have a different complex to worry Americans: the education-community-political complex. If public education fails to morph into a fully functioning 21st century system (and then perhaps into something totally new as education becomes reconstituted), there's a good chance this united front of disparate voices will be to blame. The major entities guiding education today claim they want to improve education in these accelerated times; yet when the ideas become radical, they are often blocked by a fear of losing what is known by and comfortable to educators, community members, and politicians.

- Educators, including teachers, administrators, school boards, and national education leaders, must loosen their grip on past practices and be fully ready to transform into a new type of system.

- Community members must understand that their schools will look different and function in ways they have not seen before.

- Politicians must not be so obsessed with 20th century accountability ratings that they fail to support, fund, and encourage new, broadened outcomes that more adequately prepare students to enter the global economy.

And there are other key players: the massive testing companies that provide the assessments given to students. What role will these behemoths play? America spends at least $1.7 billion each year on standardized testing (Ujifusa). These companies will not leave the stage quietly; they will try to shape any changes in the system to fit their needs.

We need visionary, articulate leaders and state and national politicians to put the interests of the students and nation before profits and ideology. We need more leaders like Ike; maybe we could create a hologram of him warning America of the education-community-political complex.

And play it continuously for everyone to hear.

Barrier 2: The Impact of Stress and School Leadership Turnover

If America's public school administrators are going to transition to local global leadership and successfully lead their schools into an age of hyper-change, then the current view of the administrative landscape must change. Most school administrators work well beyond 40 hours per week; they often spend an additional 20 to 30 hours each week working in their offices after school, monitoring after-school or evening activities, and working on weekends. This creates another obstacle for school leaders as they transition to the future: overcoming stress and burnout.

Consider the recent trends of American administrator longevity. According to a study by the School Leaders Network,

- 50% of all principals do not return to their schools after their third year,

- the turnover rate among school principals is among the highest of all professions,

- principal turnover can affect student performance by up to 25%,

- the turnover rate costs American schools $163 million each year, and

- turnover rate is even more acute in high-poverty districts: Principals are twice as likely to leave in their first 6 years ("CHURN: The High Cost of Principal Turnover").

That's 25,000 principals *each year* who are walking away from their schools—or being pushed out ("CHURN: The High Cost of Principal Turnover").

School superintendents are also in highly vulnerable positions. We know the tenure of urban superintendents is low, around 3.1 years (*Urban School Superintendents*), and the turnover rate of suburban and rural superintendents is not much better.

Teachers are feeling tremendous stress, and some studies show that up to half of all teachers leave the profession within 5 years of starting their career. Salaries are part of the reason, but the main driver is the set of unfavorable conditions the teachers encounter on their campuses, particularly a decrease in classroom autonomy and a rise in student discipline issues (Phillips). Put another way, teachers are forced to teach standards in a specific way to prepare students for the standardized testing that has come about because of the education reform disruption, and they are encountering Gen Z students who are less inclined to be regimented and are coming out of homes with less structure than in the past and from a society that no longer values public education the way it did before.

Our principals, superintendents, and teachers are so stressed they are leaving in large numbers, and their working conditions do not show any sign of improving in an era of hyper-change. Conditions will probably become *more difficult* in the transition into hyper-change.

Barrier 3: Creating Education Positions That Are Sustainable

America's teaching force has become America's largest occupation (Phillips). We have to think differently if we are to retain educators and help this hugely significant workforce transition to an era of hyper-change. Educators of all types need mentors, additional personnel to assist them with managing disruptions, the freedom to be entrepreneurial, assistance from parents and community members, and new leadership and operational structures that must be developed to manage and thrive in hyper-change.

School principals and assistant principals cannot be realistically asked to add hyper-change leadership to an already overcrowded day without adjusting other parts of their jobs. To assist campus leaders, their overall 21st century job descriptions and expectations must be changed.

- Administrators must be freed from the grind of after-hour monitoring of extracurricular events.

- Administrators who are at the forefront of leading staff into hyper-change should not be managing student discipline.

- The current school evaluation systems, with their onerous testing responsibilities, must be shifted away from administrators or eliminated.

- Administrators must be allowed to leave campus on a regular basis with mentors, teachers, or other personnel to brainstorm, think creatively, and design new systems.

- Administrator evaluations should be centered on leading in hyper-change, not the activities and responsibilities of the 20th century.

- Administrators need more time off; they must have more vacation time and personal leave.

- Instead of losing high-achieving administrators forever, they should be treated as tenured university professors and given semester-long or year-long sabbaticals.

How could these changes be achieved? As technology becomes cheaper and more plentiful, it will change duties, school operations, and money allocation. And school boards, teaching staff, and communities must commit to being part of the team that reenvisions the tasks, hours, and stress endured by school leaders. We must shift our view of the school leader from a 20th century lens to a 21st century lens.

Consider this: Teachers who spend 35 years in one school could easily have *10 different principals* during their careers. Some teachers will have even more. How many businesses can prosper with this kind of leadership turnover? What's happening here? How can so many people who take principal jobs with such enthusiasm be so eager to leave in 3 years or be pushed out the door by the community or the teachers?

And what does this turnover rate cost in dollars? Around $163 million annually when you consider preparation, hiring processes, signing bonuses, and mentoring ("CHURN: The High Cost of Principal Turnover"). Isn't there some way to invest that money proactively in saving our principals?

The same ideas should be applied to our superintendents. The main focus of the jobs should be to serve the community and to lead the transition into a new type of system. It will continue to be incredibly stressful as they balance national and state demands, community concerns, and all the 21st century disruptions impacting them daily. They, too, need time to reflect, recharge, and find emotional and physical support.

MOVING OUT OF FUTURE SHOCK: PAUSING AND BALANCING

Educators are not alone in feeling 21st century stress.

In 2017, the Game Innovation Lab at the University of Southern California School of Cinematic Arts reported it is finishing a 10-year project to develop a game titled *Walden: The Video Game*. It is based on Henry David Thoreau's idealistic, simple experiences at Walden Pond in 1854. Most video games feature cartoon characters or action figures doing amazing things, but this one focuses on the opposite: It is designed to allow its players to slow down and find balance in their lives (Peterson). Instead of saving the world or blowing up space ships, players can build a cabin, watch birds, chat with neighbors, read, and reflect on nature. The object is to be still (Pogrebin).

So, as people move into hyper-change, they want to slip back 163 years in history to a simpler time. There are so many accelerations in their lives today, they are seeking ways to live quietly.

And of course they're using technology to do it.

Perhaps we should buy this game for all school leaders to sink into as they guide their schools into the turbulent seas of hyper-change. We speak of the need to help school leaders develop futuristic mindsets, but it's time to help school leaders develop another part of their mindsets, one that helps them find new ways to slow down in an accelerating world. To move out of future shock, educators must understand the past, present, and future of schools—and they must develop the personal emotional strengths to carry them through an unpredictable future in jobs that have become among the most demanding in any profession. They must stay in touch with the parts of the educator's soul that drove them to be educators. We have spent decades teaching them to develop their schools; now we must give them the tools to develop themselves emotionally.

One recent online article offers a number of suggestions from principals to their peers for managing stress: Spend time with students, listen to music, do different kinds of new activities, read, try not to take school stress home, listen to inspirational tapes, and talk about your stress (Boyadjian et al.). The American Psychological Association offers several tips for relieving modern stress: take a break, exercise, get social support, and meditate.

Can we incorporate some of these ideas into our school leadership structures? Can we give administrators more time off each week, each month, and each year? Can we give them access to gyms for exercise? Provide suggestions on healthy diets for people who work long hours and endure great levels of stress? Arrange yoga classes or other activities for them? Should we provide them counseling and more opportunities to decompress and share their ideas and emotions? School leaders are extremely mission driven; how can we help them reach into their inner core to stay connected with that part of them that drove them to be school leaders? How can we offer meditation or reflection opportunities?

These are not trivial questions in an era when the data suggest there is rapid burnout and the job changes will continue to accelerate. New answers are urgently needed. These administrators will soon have some of the toughest leadership jobs in the world: leading schools into uncharted territory when the majority of the stakeholders are still clinging to the past.

One leader who understands the complexity of these jobs is David Manning, a former administrator with deep experience in mentoring school leaders. He has seen the changes that have enveloped schools.

David Manning, Former Administrator
San Miguel de Allende, Mexico

I have been coaching principals while in semi-retirement for the past 11 years. I started my career in education in 1971. I am a lifelong educator and I take pride in that. So many things have changed, but there are some basic issues that have not changed.

Educational leaders are still dealing with what we called "time management" over 30 years ago. There are more demands on principals because of the technological advances such as e-mail and social media. Many districts require that principals respond to parent e-mails and requests within 24 hours. This kind of accessibility to the principal adds to the workload and the work time, not to mention stress. Many administrators, especially high school principals, have Twitter accounts and feel they are necessary to stay connected to their students. Technology can also bring new kinds of issues that administrators did not deal with years ago. The rise of bullying, inappropriate postings/pictures, selfies, all are issues that can add to the busy days of administrators, causing disruptions that have to be handled and can distract from the focus on instruction and a safe orderly environment. Keeping a calm demeanor and using skilled communication techniques are more necessary than ever for the administrator to be able to handle these issues effectively and efficiently. Leadership training must include developing these traits and skills.

I believe mindfulness and reflection will be more important in the future. I also think that leadership training will need to be focused on these concepts more than ever before. The artistic, symbolic, and spiritual side of leadership will be more important than ever in the future.

The issue of life/work balance comes up as a goal in almost all of my new clients who are in school leadership positions. Most principals realize the value of their lives outside of the school building and the importance of family time. There is no magic wand that would reduce the demands on the principal. In fact, there are more demands than ever these days.

Manning has some advice for today's harried school leaders. He advises administrators to pause, to seek "still points" each day when they can take deep breaths and calm their thoughts. He urges them to find "stop-overs," which could range from an hour to multiple days. These are times when administrators escape the job and focus on "being" and not "doing." And he advises them to get away from time to time for what he calls "grinding halts," which might be weeks or months away from the job or during transitions between jobs.

Manning also reminds us that while principals and superintendents may lead with best educational practices, they also lead with their souls.

I once heard a wonderful principal say that education is "holy work." That kind of language seems to frighten many traditional educators. However, we are in the business of caring for, while they are with us during that school day, and educating the whole child.

To discuss this more, I believe we need to acknowledge that most educational leaders become leaders to make an impact on more students, teachers, parents, and their community. It is truly a mission, rather than a job. They put their heart and soul into it. They realize the demands of high-stakes testing and want to balance this with the deeper needs of their students and staff. Some say this "heart and soul" rhetoric is not appropriate in the school setting, but I wholeheartedly disagree. I can give many examples of coaching principals who bring personal issues as well as professional issues to the coaching conversations. Our lives can be messy and development can be nonlinear. Who you are as a person and who you are as a leader are interconnected so tightly that neither can be ignored. As a coach, it would be dishonorable of me to tell the leader I am coaching that they cannot talk about a difficult personal issue in their life. I ask my coaching clients to create four to five goals when they begin coaching with me, and one of them can be a personal goal.

Is wanting more work and life balance personal or professional? It is both.

We cannot separate the principals or superintendents from who they are as individuals. To be great leaders, they must find purpose in their profession and a preponderance of joy in what they do. If we don't shift our thinking on how we view and support our leaders, the turnover rate in school leadership will prevent the full transformations to the next level of 21st century schooling.

TIPS FOR HELPING TEACHERS: MINDFULNESS, BALANCE, AND RESPECT

As a sign of our accelerated times, many national conferences now have breakout sessions to help educators develop mindfulness techniques. Brandi Lust is a former teacher and instructional coach whose business, Learning Lab Consulting in Columbus, Ohio, facilitates learning experiences using mindfulness and social and emotional learning as tools toward health and wholeness. In this era of hyper-change, schools are realizing they need new approaches to assist staff members, so they are reaching out to her for assistance.

She has some valuable advice for administrators as they lead teachers in these accelerated times.

Stories From Exceptional Educational Leaders

Brandi Lust, Founder
Learning Lab Consulting
Columbus, Ohio

When I was a teacher, I often felt overwhelmed, underappreciated, and isolated. My first year I taught 185 high school students English every day, which left me little time to engage with colleagues. When I left work, I went home exhausted and with few emotional resources to give my family. By my fifth year, I had four different courses I taught daily. I was responsible for publishing a 200-page book once a year as the yearbook adviser, and I was a teacher-partner for Pages, a rigorous creative writing program funded through an art center in Columbus. At the same time, no one above me seemed to notice. The only recognition I still remember from that time was when an assistant principal, who was also very stressed, came into my classroom waving grade cards in her hand, which I had forgotten in my mailbox. With a tone of exasperated frustration on her face, she slammed them on my desk and then tossed her hands up in the air in front of a classroom of students. I was mortified.

Having first-hand experience with stress and the emotional impact of working in schools, I believe that mindfulness and social and emotional learning should be an integrated part of educational environments. Research confirms this. In the issue brief Teacher Stress and Health: Effects on Teachers, Students and Schools, *it states that 46% of educators report high levels of daily stress, which ties teaching with nursing as the most stressful profession. According to the report, teacher stress has been shown to be detrimental to educators' health and well-being and is also linked to negative effects on student social adjustment and achievement.*

I think many recognize that this system is unsustainable. At the same time, making the shift is not easy. Districts have to make the choice to invest in the health of staff and get communities to support their decision at a time when the culture of education is to bypass the teacher for the sake of serving student needs.

Lust provides learning experiences about mindfulness training and emotional learning through research-based tools to help educators be more mindful, connected, compassionate, and growth-oriented. Her goal is to engage the whole person. She's found teachers and administrators to be very receptive.

Teachers are grateful to have professional development that is applicable and accessible, while still recognizing their humanity and the emotional needs of staff and students. Administrators are pleased to have the opportunity to bring humanitarian values back into education and provide development that meets educator and school needs in an innovative manner.

One challenge to implementing mindfulness and reflective practices with educators is the pervasive culture of time scarcity. To ask educators and administrators to give even 10 minutes a day to mindfulness practice, even if spending that 10 minutes has been shown to have tremendous mental and physical health benefits, is a tough sell. I think this is because we view time as a dwindling resource—something we don't have enough of. This changes the way we make decisions, and we favor short-term gains over long-term consequences. Self-care, mindfulness, and other reflective practices take time, require slowing down, and don't have the same immediacy of other demands. Without them, however, the work is unsustainable and quality of life and relationships decreases.

(Continued)

(Continued)

Another challenge in implementing mindfulness and other reflective practices that involve social and emotional learning is that it's a very new idea to bring stillness, quiet, reflection, and vulnerability into public space, and specifically into the field of education. Whenever you are doing something new, it takes time to build support and understanding. Right now I would say I am working with early adopters, and I am hoping the results will gain the interest of others and grow the work.

Lust has these words of advice for school leaders as they move forward:

- *I would encourage leaders who wish to introduce mindfulness to staff to develop a personal mindfulness practice before or alongside those whom they serve.*

- *I would also discourage school leaders from viewing mindfulness as a silver bullet. It is an amazing tool, maybe even life changing, but it needs to be used alongside genuine conversation about the tremendous stress that teachers and administrators face each day and supported by actions taken individually and in community to build resilience and create sustainability.*

- *Teachers need to hear from leadership that they are valuable people doing difficult work. That it is okay not to take work home every day. They need to hear that they should not sacrifice their family relationships for the sake of their job, and that deciding not to grade the essay they collected last week is a good choice if it means that they are choosing their health and mental well-being.*

- *In addition, teachers need time and space to connect, not to collaborate, but to process the experiences they face daily. While this may seem like a "waste of time" in this educational season's obsession with measurements and accountability, processing together can be a source of common humanity and increased resilience. Much of the harm of stress comes from when it isolates us from others.*

- *To this end, personal development has to be a component of professional development. Resources like mindfulness, gratitude, growth, connection, compassion, and resilience can be taught, and the best way to teach them is to have authentically grappled with and engaged those resources personally.*

Lust also advises administrators to be mindful listeners to empower teachers and address their needs. "Leaders need to listen carefully and closely to what educators have to say about their own experiences," she says. "This will be a starting place for the work that is to come."

LET'S BE APPLE AND MICROSOFT

Finally, imagine if Steve Jobs of Apple and Bill Gates of Microsoft, two of the world's most successful and innovative corporate leaders, had been school leaders. Could they have still changed the world?

Like most school leaders, Jobs and Gates exhibited passion, endurance, talent, and dedication in their fields. But unlike school leaders, they weren't controlled by political systems or stakeholders who refused to let go of the status quo. Of course they overcame many other challenges, including starting companies that would lead the world into new areas. They had unique visions they were able to put into place.

Will school leaders emulate Jobs and Gates in their daring and leadership? Or will they view the world through a restricted lens that goes only as far as the next standardized test?

Principals and superintendents don't need to have the unique, laser-like vision of Gates and Jobs; there is abundant research about accelerations available to guide them, and the trends in students, technology, and societal disruptions are all around them to see. They need flexibility and new levels of support to implement the vision—along with a willingness to lead stakeholders into the unknown. They need to cope, adjust, and transform through 21st century disruptions so their schools will slip quickly into the new model that is just beyond the horizon.

It's time for local and national educator leaders to step to the forefront and prepare their staff, parents, community members, and policymakers for hyper-change in education. They don't need to worry about the students transforming with them; they're already there waiting. Principals and superintendents must move from being passive participants to active trendsetters. As they lead schools in disruptive times, they must shape an education future that blends local needs with global readiness.

They must be leaders for the 21st century.

Digitization, Disruption, and Democratization

1. Look in your own community for examples of businesses that have been digitized, disrupted, and then democratized.

2. Can you find any examples of the digitization, disruption, and democratization occurring in your school?

3. How will you involve your stakeholders in shifting into digitization, disruption, and democratization?

4. What will be the role of teachers, curriculum, and administrators when students can interact with AI, holograms, and VR?

5. How do you think this shift from a formal structure to more of an independent system will affect students emotionally?

6. As schools become more democratized and learning spaces become more dispersed, how much time should be provided in school or some other setting for students to socialize and develop their interaction skills?

7. What new ethical issues will students encounter as they become more dependent on stronger and wider-reaching technology?

8. The arts in schools fill a vital creative void for students; what will be their place and that of other electives in a democratized education environment?

9. How should schools continue to transform their classrooms to make use of more technology and the learning skills of this generation and future generations who will be growing up with deeper technology skills and new expectations?

Reshaping Your Job to Manage Hyper-Stress

10. If you could reshape your job to manage hyper-stress, what would you do?

11. Are you finding time to pause? To have still points and stop-overs? When's the last time you had a grinding halt?

12. Will you be able to implement any sort of innovative practices, like mindfulness in professional development, to help teachers deal with hyper-stress.

13. What else can you do to value teachers experiencing hyper-change?

References

A Nation at Risk. Archived. U.S. Department of Education, April 1983. Web. 20 Nov. 2016.

Adams, Aleta Eberett. Personal communication. 09 Jan. 2017.

Adrean, Angie. Personal communication. 25 July 2016.

Albert Shanker Institute. "A Look at Teacher Diversity." *American Educator* 40 (2016): 18–19, 43. Web. 28 Oct. 2016.

Barker, Kristin. "Road Tested/The Truth About Millennial Teachers." *Education Update: The Elephant (and Donkey) in the Room* 57 (Oct. 2015). Web. 28 Oct. 2016.

Barnes, Robert, and Moriah Balingit. "Supreme Court Takes Up School Bathroom Rules for Transgender Students." *Washington Post*, 28 Oct. 2016. Web. 19 Feb. 2017.

Bell, Keith. Personal communication. 09 Feb. 2017.

Bennett, Meegan. Personal communication. 23 Jan. 2017.

Bhatia, Sameer. "5 Surprising Ways Cloud Computing Is Changing Education." *Cloud Tweaks,* 03 December 2014. Web. 01 June 2017.

Bowie, David. *Changes.* EMI, 1990. CD.

Boyadjian, Lucie, et al. "Principals Offer 30 Ways to Fight Stress." *Education World,* n.d. Web. 24 Feb. 2017.

Brown, Emma. "As Immigration Resurges, U.S. Public Schools Help Children Find Their Footing." *Washington Post,* 07 Feb. 2016. Web. 19 Feb. 2017.

Brown, Emma. "On the Anniversary of Brown v. Board, New Evidence That U.S. Schools Are Resegregating." *Washington Post,* 17 May 2014. Web. 28 Oct. 2016.

Camera, Lauren. "The New Segregation." *U.S. News & World Report*, 26 July 2016. Web. 20 Feb. 2017.

"CHURN: The High Cost of Principal Turnover." *Principals Changing Public Education.* School Leaders Network, 2014. Web. 29 Jan. 2017.

CNBC. "Meet the 2015 CNBC Disruptor 50 Companies." CNBC.com, 02 Feb. 2016. Web. 9 Apr. 2017.

Crockett, Ross. "28 Life Skills That Define Student Readiness [Infographic]." *Global Digital Citizen Foundation*, 18 Feb. 2017. Web. 18 Feb. 2017.

Daggett, Bill E., EdD. *Preparing Our Students for Their Futures: WHY Innovative Practices Are Needed*. International Center for Leadership in Education, Jan. 2017. Web. 1 June 2017.

Dols, Paul. Personal communication. 31 Dec. 2016.

Dooley, Erin. "Obama to Public Schools: Allow Transgender Students Access to Bathrooms." *ABC News*. ABC News Network, 13 May 2016. Web. 19 Feb. 2017.

Doorley, Scott, and Scott Witthoft. *Make a Space: How to Set the Stage for Creative Collaboration*. John Wiley & Sons, 2012.

Dostal, Jay, PhD. Personal communication. 29 Dec. 2016.

"Eisenhower Warns of Military-Industrial Complex." *History.com*. A&E Television Networks, n.d. Web. 29 Dec. 2016.

"Fast Facts." National Center for Education Statistics, n.d. Web. 30 Dec. 2016.

Finnamore, Chris, and David Ludlow. "Top Inventions and Technical Innovations of World War 2." *Expert Reviews*, 01 May 2015. Web. 01 June 2017.

Freeland, Chrystia. "Al Gore and the Age of Hyper-Change." *Reuters*. Thomson Reuters, 27 Feb. 2013. Web. 20 Nov. 2016.

Friedman, Nick. "Making the Most of Millennial Teacher Mindsets." *Getting Smart*, 13 Feb. 2015. Web. 28 Oct. 2016.

Friedman, Thomas L. *Thank You for Being Late: An Optimist's Guide to Thriving in the Age of Accelerations*. New York: Farrar, Straus and Giroux, 2016.

Fuller, Buckminster. *Critical Path*. New York: St. Martin's Griffin, 1982.

Galloway, Patrick. Personal communication. 05 Feb. 2017.

Gandara, Patricia. "The Latino Education Crisis." *Educational Leadership* 67 (Feb. 2010): 24–30. Web. 19 Feb. 2017.

Ganim, Sara, and Linh Tran. "Trump's Choice for Education Secretary Raises Questions." Cable News Network, 02 Dec. 2016. Web. 30 Dec. 2016.

Godin, Seth. "A Ten Year Plan Is Absurd." *Seth's Blog*, 5 June 2016. Web.

Grawer, Kevin, PhD. Personal communication. 08 Jan. 2017.

Greenberg, M.T., et al. "Teacher Stress and Health." *RWFJF*, Robert Woods Johnson Foundation, 1 Sept. 2016.

Hadad, Chuck. "#Being13: Teens and Social Media." Cable News Network, 13 Oct. 2015. Web. 03 June 2017.

"Homeschooling." *Fast Facts*. National Center for Education Statistics, n.d. Web. 19 Feb. 2017.

ISTE Connects. "8 Classroom Uses for Holographic Technology." *ISTE*, 22 Jan. 2015. Web. 23 Jan. 2017.

Jackson, Carrie. Personal communication. 09 Feb. 2017.

Janzen, Rod. "Melting Pot or Mosaic?" *Educational Leadership: Educating for Diversity* 51 (May 1994): 9–11. Web. 19 Feb. 2017.

Jose, Jack M. Personal communication. 21 Jan. 2017.

Jukes, Ian. "Tweets With Replies by Ian Jukes (@ijukes)." Twitter, 23 Feb. 2017. Web. 25 Feb. 2017.

Kaste, Martin. "Futurist 40 Years Later: Possibilities, Not Predictions." *All Things Considered*, NPR, 26 July 2010. Web. 01 June 2017.

Larson, Lotta. "Beyond Your Classroom's Walls." *Educational Leadership: The Global-Ready Student* 74 (Dec. 2016/Jan. 2017). Web. 11 Feb. 2017.

Lehmann, Chris. Personal communication. 09 Feb. 2017.

"Like Walking Through a Hailstorm": Discrimination Against LGBT Youth in Schools. Human Rights Watch, 07 Dec. 2016. Web. 20 Feb. 2017.

Litvinov, Amanda. "Trump Hate Rhetoric Fuels Rise in School Racial, Ethnic Tensions: Educator Survey." *Education Votes*. National Education Association, 18 Apr. 2016. Web. 19 Feb. 2017.

Liu, Joseph. "Religion in the Public Schools." *Pew Research Center's Religion & Public Life Project*, 09 May 2007. Web. 19 Feb. 2017.

Luckin, Rose, Wayne Holmes, Mark Griffiths, and Laurie B. Forcier. *Intelligence Unleashed: An Argument for AI in Education.* London: Pearson and UCL Knowledge Lab, University College, 2016. Web. 29 Jan. 2017.

Lust, Brandi. Personal communication. 22 Dec. 2016.

Manning, David. Personal communication. 01 Jan. 2017.

Markey, Jason. Personal communication. 25 Nov. 2016.

Maxwell, Lesli A. "U.S. School Enrollment Hits Majority-Minority Milestone." *Education Week* 34 (19 Aug. 2014): 1, 12, 14–15. Web. 28 Oct. 2016.

McCoy, Derek. Personal communication. 09 Feb. 2017.

"Moore's Law." *Encyclopedia Britannica.* Encyclopedia Britannica, Inc., 17 Nov. 2015. Web. 16 Apr. 2017.

Morris, Gregg. Personal communication. 27 July 2016.

Novak, Jill, PhD. "Six Generations Live in America Today." American Association of University Women: Dearborn (MI) Branch, 22 May 2012. Web. 03 June 2017.

Orwell, George. *1984.* Toronto, Ontario: Harper Perennial Classics, 1949.

Peterson, Britt. "Can a Video Game Capture the Magic of Walden?" *Smithsonian.com.* Smithsonian Institution, 01 Mar. 2017. Web. 25 Feb. 2017.

Phillips, Owen. "Revolving Door of Teachers Costs Schools Billions Every Year." *NPR.* NPR, 30 Mar. 2015. Web. 29 Jan. 2017.

Pogrebin, Robin. "In 'Walden' Video Game, the Challenge Is Stillness." *New York Times*, 24 Feb. 2017. Web. 25 Feb. 2017.

Powell, Alvin. "How Sputnik Changed U.S. Education." *Harvard Gazette*, 11 Oct. 2007.

Prensky, Marc. "Our Brains Extended." *Educational Leadership: Technology-Rich Learning* 70 (Mar. 2013): 22–27. Web. 24 Feb. 2017.

"Preparing Students for the World: Final Report of the State Board of Education's Task Force on Global Education." North Carolina State Board of Education, Jan. 2013. Web. 18 Feb. 2017.

Reede, Elizabeth, and Larissa Bailiff. "When Virtual Reality Meets Education." *TechCrunch*, 23 Jan. 2016. Web. 08 Jan. 2017.

Regelski, Jennifer, PhD. Personal communication. 02 Feb. 2017.

Richardson, Will. "Getting Schools Ready for the World." *Educational Leadership: The Global-Ready Student* 74 (Dec. 2016/Jan. 2016): 24–29. Web. 11 Feb. 2017.

Robinson, Ken (with Lou Aronica). *The Element: How Finding Your Passion Changes Everything*. Camberwell, Vic.: Penguin, 2010.

Roe, Michael John. Personal communication. 05 Feb. 2017.

Rouse, Charles. Personal communication. 04 Dec. 2016.

Sass, E. "American Educational History Timeline." *Ed-Resources.com*, 26 Apr. 2017. Web. 01 June 2017.

Schilling, David Russell. "Knowledge Doubling Every 12 Months, Soon to Be Every 12 Hours." *Industry Tap*, 13 Dec. 2013. Web. 18 Apr. 2017.

Sebach, Gary. Personal communication. 10 Jan. 2017.

Secretary's Commission on Achieving Necessary Skills. "What Work Requires of Schools: A SCANS Report for America 2000." U.S. Department of Labor, n.d. Web. 26 Dec. 2016.

Sharfin, Ira. Personal communication. 29 Jan. 2017.

Sinek, Simon. *Leaders Eat Last: Why Some Teams Pull Together and Others Don't*. London: Portfolio/Penguin, 2014.

Taylor, Krista L. Personal communication. 21 Jan. 2017.

Thoma, Kate. Personal communication. 05 Feb. 2017.

Toffler, Alvin. *Future Shock*. New York: Bantam, 1970.

Toffler, Alvin, and Heidi Toffler. *The Third Wave*. New York: Bantam, 1980.

Toppo, Greg, and Paul Overberg. "Diversity in the Classroom: Sides Square Off in Minnesota." *USA Today*, 18 Mar. 2015. Web. 19 Feb. 2017.

Ujifusa, Andrew. "Standardized Testing Costs States $1.7 Billion a Year, Study Says." *Education Week*, 11 May 2016. Web. 25 Feb. 2017.

Urban School Superintendents: Characteristics, Tenure, and Salary. Second Biennial Survey. Washington, DC: Council of the Great City Schools, 2000. Web. 29 Jan. 2017.

Waldrop, M. Mitchell. "The Chips Are Down for Moore's Law." *Nature News*, 09 Feb. 2016. Web. 01 June 2017.

Walker, Todd A., PhD. Personal communication. 05 Feb. 2017.

Wallace, Kelly. "Teens Spend 9 Hours a Day Using Media, Report Says." *CNN*, 03 Nov. 2015. Web. 18 Feb. 2017.

White, Rae L., PhD. Personal communication. 19 Feb. 2017.

Wittman, William L. E-mail interview. 09 Jan. 2017.

Wolchover, Natalie. "What Is the Future of Computers?" *LiveScience*, 10 Sept. 2012. Web. 01 June 2017.

Woolf, Steve. Personal communication. 09 Feb. 2017.

Index

NOTE: Page references in *italics* refer to figures.

digitization in schools, 207–214
disruption in schools, 207–208,
    214–217
former administrator's view of
    (example), 209, 226–227
former teacher's view of (example),
    228–231
leadership for, 231
overcoming barriers of, 219–224
overview, 205–206
pausing and balancing for, 224–225

IBM, 17
Immigration, political issues of, 143.
    See also Diversity
Implementation timeline, for
    improvement plans, 196
Industrial Revolution, disruption
    from, 6–8
Intelligence Unleashed (Pearson),
    211–212
International Center for Leadership in
    Education, 130–132
International language
    instruction, 124
International Society for Technology
    in Education (ISTE), 213–214
International travel, 125
Internet, technology disruption from,
    60–61
"Ivory tower syndrome," 86

Jackson, Carrie, 209
Jiminez, Sandra, 144
Jobs, Steve, 231
Jose, Jack, 88–90

Kearney (Nebraska) High School,
    85–87
Knowledge
    accelerating speed of, 15–18, *18*
    acquisition of, with technology,
        63–65
Knowledge about students,
    safety and, 53
Kurzweil, Ray, 16

"Labels," for students, 84
Language instruction, 124

Leaders Eat Last (Sinek), 37
Leadership
    assessment and, 195
    for Hyper-Change Age, 231
    local global leaders, 33–35
    overcoming turnover problem in,
        221–222
    stakeholders' common vision, 195
Leander (Texas) High School,
    121–122
Learning environment consultant's
    view (example), on generational
    differences, 109–111
Learning Lab Consulting, 228–231
Learning space planning, for
    generational differences, 109–116
Legal issues
    law enforcement and student safety, 53
    litigious nature of society, 27
    public records requests, 168–169
Lehmann, Chris, 125–127
LGBT rights, diversity issues and,
    155–157. *See also* Diversity
Lifelong learning, for global readiness,
    123, 130–132
"Like Walking Through a Hailstorm"
    (Human Rights Watch), 155–156
Local global leaders, 33–35
Lust, Brandi, 228–231

Mann, Horace, 6
Manning, David, 225–227
Maplewood Richmond Heights High
    School (St. Louis, Missouri),
    43–50
Marian University (Indianapolis),
    93–95
Markey, Jason, 71–73
McCoy, Derek, 73–75
Measurement, for assessing progress,
    189–190
Media relations, for schools, 168,
    171–172
Mental health, student safety and,
    48–50
Messaging
    feedback for, 169–170
    systems of, 165–167
    See also Transparency

CORWIN LEADERSHIP

**Simon T. Bailey &
Marceta F. Reilly**
On providing a simple,
sustainable framework
that will help you
move your school from
mediocrity to brilliance.

Edie L. Holcomb
Use data to construct
an equitable learning
environment, develop
instruction, and
empower effective
PL communities.

**Debbie Silver &
Dedra Stafford**
Equip educators to
develop resilient and
mindful learners primed
for academic growth
and personal success.

**Peter Gamwell
& Jane Daly**
A fresh perspective
on how to nurture
creativity, innovation,
leadership, and
engagement.

**Steven Katz,
Lisa Ain Dack,
& John Malloy**
Leverage the oppositional
forces of top-down
expectations and bottom-
up experience to create
an intelligent, responsive
school.

**Lyn Sharratt &
Beate Planche**
A resource-rich guide that
provides a strategic path
to achieving sustainable
communities of deep
learners.

Peter M. DeWitt
Meet stakeholders where
they are, motivate them
to improve, and model how
to do it.

Leadership that Makes an Impact

Charlotte Danielson
Harness the power of informal professional conversation and invite teachers to boost achievement.

Liz Wiseman, Lois Allen, & Elise Foster
Use leadership to bring out the best in others—liberating staff to excel and doubling your team's effectiveness.

Eric Sheninger
Use digital resources to create a new school culture, increase engagement, and facilitate real-time PD.

Russell J. Quaglia, Michael J. Corso, & Lisa L. Lande
Listen to your school's voice to see how you can increase engagement, involvement, and academic motivation.

Michael Fullan, Joanne Quinn, & Joanne McEachen
Learn the right drivers to mobilize complex, coherent, whole-system change and transform learning for all students.

CORWIN

A SAGE Publishing Company

Helping educators make the greatest impact

CORWIN HAS ONE MISSION: to enhance education through intentional professional learning.

We build long-term relationships with our authors, educators, clients, and associations who partner with us to develop and continuously improve the best evidence-based practices that establish and support lifelong learning.

THE PROFESSIONAL LEARNING ASSOCIATION

Learning Forward is a nonprofit, international membership association of learning educators committed to one vision in K–12 education: Excellent teaching and learning every day. To realize that vision, Learning Forward pursues its mission to build the capacity of leaders to establish and sustain highly effective professional learning. Information about membership, services, and products is available from www.learningforward.org.

Solutions you want. Experts you trust. Results you need.

AUTHOR CONSULTING

Author Consulting

On-site professional learning with sustainable results! Let us help you design a professional learning plan to meet the unique needs of your school or district. www.corwin.com/pd

INSTITUTES

Institutes

Corwin Institutes provide collaborative learning experiences that equip your team with tools and action plans ready for immediate implementation. www.corwin.com/institutes

ECOURSES

eCourses

Practical, flexible online professional learning designed to let you go at your own pace. www.corwin.com/ecourses

READ2EARN

Read2Earn

Did you know you can earn graduate credit for reading this book? Find out how: www.corwin.com/read2earn

Contact an account manager at (800) 831-6640 or visit **www.corwin.com** for more information.

CORWIN